THE BELIEVER'S AUTHORITY IN THE EARTH

Michael E.B. Maher

Unless otherwise indicated, all Scripture quotations in this teaching are from the *New King James Version* of the bible.

Revised Edition 2023

ISBN: 978-0639943213

Books by Michael E.B. Maher

Foundation Doctrines of Christ

Repentance from Dead Works
Faith Toward God
Doctrine of Baptisms
Laying on of Hands
Resurrection of the Dead
Eternal Judgement

Man, the Image of God

The Will of Man
The Spirit of Man
The Conscience of Man
The Mind of Man
The Body of Man

Gifts of the Church

Spiritual Gifts
Ministry Gifts
The Revelation Gifts
The Power Gifts
The Speaking Gifts

End of the Ages

The Last Three Superpowers
The Last Days
The Seventh Seal
The Millennial Kingdom

The End of the Age

Standalone

There is Sin to Death
Prayer
Being Unforgiving
Being led by the Spirit
Born Free from Sin
The Two Gospels Explained
Being led by the Spirit
Of Such is the Kingdom
Rich through His Poverty
Suffering as a Christian
Growing Strong in Spirit
The Believer's Authority in the Earth
The Prayer of Faith
Predestined to His Purpose
Holy Spirit Encounters
The Bible Creation Account
The Blood of Christ
The Church and the State

Contents

Chapter 1	1
The church's adversary	1
The god of this world	1
The church's adversary	9
Chapter 2	15
How Jesus destroyed the devil	15
The deceiver was deceived	15
Satan killed Jesus	30
Why Jesus went to Hades	34
Jesus' authority	44
Chapter 3	49
Our authority over the devil	49
Jesus delegated His authority	49
The believer's weapons	52
We must exercise our authority	56
Our sphere of authority	58
Resisting the devil	65
Using God's word	69
Chapter 4	77
Dealing with our adversary	77
Satan's devices	77
Satan is persistent	80
Satan is a dignitary	81

The church's adversary

Chapter 1
The church's adversary

The god of this world

Isaiah 14:3-17 *"It shall come to pass in the day the Lord gives you rest from your sorrow, and from your fear and the hard bondage in which you were made to serve, (4) that you will take up this proverb against the king of Babylon, and say: "How the oppressor has ceased, The golden city ceased! (5) The Lord has broken the staff of the wicked, the sceptre of the ruler; (6) He who struck the people in wrath with a continual stroke, He who ruled the nations in anger, is persecuted and no one hinders. (7) The whole earth is at rest and quiet; they break forth into singing. (8) Indeed the cypress trees rejoice over you, and the cedars of Lebanon, Saying, 'Since you were cut down, No woodsman has come up against us.' (9) "Hell from beneath is excited about you, to meet you at your coming; It stirs up the dead for you, All the chief ones of the earth; It has raised up from their thrones All the kings of the nations. (10) They all shall speak and say to you: 'Have you also become as weak as we? Have you become like us? (11) Your pomp is brought down to Sheol, and the sound of your stringed instruments; the maggot is spread under you, and worms cover you.' (12) "How you are fallen from heaven, O Lucifer, son of the morning! How you are cut down to the ground, you who weakened the nations! (13)*

The church's adversary

For you have said in your heart: 'I will ascend into heaven, I will exalt my throne above the stars of God; I will also sit on the mount of the congregation On the farthest sides of the north; (14) I will ascend above the heights of the clouds, I will be like the Most High.' (15) Yet you shall be brought down to Sheol, to the lowest depths of the Pit. (16) "Those who see you will gaze at you, And consider you, saying: 'Is this the man who made the earth tremble, Who shook kingdoms, (17) Who made the world as a wilderness And destroyed its cities, Who did not open the house of his prisoners?"

In this section we want to discuss the biblical truth that Satan is the god of this world and what the ramifications of that truth are. Many people ask the question that if God is love then why is there so much pain and suffering in the world? As we will see in this section, the answer to that question is that God is not the God of this world, but rather Satan is. The above quoted passage of scripture referring to the King of Babylon is in fact referring to Satan. We know that because the Lord calls the King of Babylon, Lucifer and describes to us the event that took place when the Archangel Lucifer made his attempt to become like God. And so in this passage the Lord reveals a number of truths to us about Satan. Firstly, we see that Satan is indeed the ruler of this world, for this passage describes him as the ruler of the nations who makes the earth tremble, shakes kingdoms, makes the world a wilderness and destroys its cities. This passage goes on to declare that the whole earth will be at rest, when Satan and his angels are finally removed from the earth. And so we can clearly see from this passage that Satan is in fact the ruler of this world. Secondly, God gives

The church's adversary

us some insight into the manner in which the devil reigns in the earth, for this passage describes him as being a wicked ruler who continually strikes the people of the earth in wrath, ruling the nations in anger, shaking kingdoms and making the whole earth tremble. This passage reveals to us that Satan's sole agenda is one of destruction, for it describes his weakening the nations, destroying their cities, and making the whole earth a wilderness. We also see that Satan is the one who initiates strife and wars between nations, for in this passage we see that once Satan and his angels are finally removed from the earth, the nations declare that no one attempts to destroy them any longer and the whole earth is quite and at rest. This brings us to the third truth revealed to us in this passage, which is the punishment that awaits Satan when he is finally removed from the earth, for this passage describes Satan's decent into the lower parts of hell to suffer torment at the end of the age. Satan and his angels know full well that they are already condemned and that they are destined for eternal destruction. And so their whole agenda for the little time they have remaining, is to destroy as much as they can and take as many people with them as they can. And so there can be no doubt that everything destructive in this world is initiated by the god of this world, which is Satan.

> *Luke 4:5-7 "Then the devil, taking Him up on a high mountain, showed Him all the kingdoms of the world in a moment of time. (6) And the devil said to Him, "All this authority I will give You, and their glory; for this has been delivered to me, and I give it to whomever I wish. (7) Therefore, if You will worship before me, all will be Yours."*

The church's adversary

We have seen in the previous passage of scripture that Satan is the god of this world. The question is then asked, how did Satan become the god of this world? To answer that question we need to go back to the events that took place in the Garden of Eden. We all know the account of how the devil tempted Adam and Eve to disobey God by eating the forbidden fruit of the "knowledge of good and evil". Adam's act of disobedience was in fact an act of rebellion against God's rule. And so in effect when Adam rebelled against God he changed his allegiance from serving God to serving the devil, and thus he delivered this world into the hands of the devil. Although Adam had no moral right to do what he did, he did have the legal right to do it because God had given him dominion over this world (Genesis 1:26). And so we see that when Adam delivered his dominion over the world into the hands of the devil, Satan then legally became the god of this world. The above quoted passage of scripture confirms this truth to us, for in this passage Satan boasted to the Lord Jesus that the authority over all the kingdoms of the world had been delivered to him and that he could give it to whoever he wished. The Lord Jesus did not dispute Satan's claim, thus acknowledging that Satan's claim was correct. And so we see that God recognises the authority that Satan holds in the earth, for he obtained it legally even though it had been obtained through Adam's treasonous act against God. So what is the nature of Satan's authority in the earth? In other words what can he do and what can he not do? All authority ultimately comes from God, and when He gives an individual authority He decides what the limits of that authority are (Romans 13:1). When God gave Adam dominion in the earth He gave him authority over all of creation. And so, we see that Satan uses his authority over

The church's adversary

creation to initiate destructive events in the earth such as hurricanes, tornados, etc (Romans 8:19-22). Although Adam's authority in the earth included every living creature on the earth there was nevertheless one exception, for God did not give Adam authority over his fellow man. The reason for that was because God created mankind for Himself. And so we see that unlike the rest of creation, the authority delivered to Satan did not automatically extend to mankind. The reason for that is because every man born into the earth is created by God with a free will, and God will not allow the free will of any man to be overridden in this life. And so in order for Satan to be able to gain authority over men, he must first get them to submit to him of their own free will. If however, men do not submit to Satan of their own free will then he has no authority over them. So how does Satan get men to submit to him of their own free will? Very simply, just as he did with Adam, he tempts them to commit sin. The simplest definition of sin is to disobey God. Sadly because all men commit sin (Romans 5:12) they therefore change their allegiance to God and submit themselves to their new god, Satan. And so we see that through their disobedience to God, all men by default willingly submit to Satan's authority. It was for that reason that the devil tried to tempt the Lord Jesus to commit sin in the wilderness. The Lord Jesus however was the only man that never sinned, thereby refusing to submit Himself to Satan's rule, which is precisely why Satan couldn't exercise authority over Jesus when He walked on the earth (John 14:30).

2 Corinthians 4:3-4 "But even if our gospel is veiled, it is veiled to those who are perishing, (4) whose minds the god of this age has blinded, who do

The church's adversary

not believe, lest the light of the gospel of the glory of Christ, who is the image of God, should shine on them."

In the passage of scripture quoted above the apostle Paul refers to Satan as the god of this age, thus confirming the truth to us that Satan is indeed the god of this world, for the word translated "age" in this passage can also be translated "world". Nevertheless the word translated "age" also reveals to us that there is a time limit to Satan's rule in the earth, for God is the one who decrees when an age begins and when it ends, and this age is very rapidly coming to an end. There are two more spiritual truths that we learn from this passage. The first truth we learn is that Satan exercises his authority over those who are perishing i.e. unbelievers, thus implying that believers do not fall under his authority. So what prohibits Satan from exercising his authority over believers? The reason is because although believers are in this world, they are not of this world and are therefore not subject to the god of this world. The second truth we learn from this passage is the method that Satan uses to exercise his authority over unbelievers, for the scripture states that He blinds their minds so that they cannot see the light or truth of the gospel. However, not only does Satan have the ability to prevent unbelievers from seeing the truth of the gospel, he also has the ability to prevent them from seeing any other truth as well. And so he is able to deceive those who are perishing into believing whatever lie he chooses, and because people always act on that which they believe, Satan is therefore able to influence people's behaviour by deceiving them into believing the lies he tells them.

The church's adversary

1 John 5:19 "We know that we are of God, and the whole world lies under the sway of the wicked one."

We have seen in the previous scripture that the method Satan uses to exercise his authority over unbelievers is to blind their minds to the truth, thus ensuring that they will believe the lie. And because people act on that which they believe, Satan is therefore able to influence their behaviour. The above quoted passage of scripture confirms that truth for us, because in this passage the apostle John teaches us that the whole world lies under the sway of the wicked one. In other words Satan has the ability to influence the behaviour of the whole world through his lies, which they believe are the truth. In this passage John also confirms the same truth as taught by the apostle Paul, i.e. that Satan has no authority over the saints and he only has authority over those who are of this world i.e. the unbelievers. For in this passage John differentiates between the saints and the rest of the world by stating that we are of God, and it is only those of this world over which the devil holds sway.

Revelation 20:1-3 "Then I saw an angel coming down from heaven, having the key to the bottomless pit and a great chain in his hand. (2) He laid hold of the dragon, that serpent of old, who is the Devil and Satan, and bound him for a thousand years; (3) and he cast him into the bottomless pit, and shut him up, and set a seal on him, so that he should deceive the nations no more till the thousand years were finished. But after these things he must be released for a little while."

The church's adversary

As revealed to us in the above quoted passage of scripture there is coming a time when Satan will be removed from this world. That event will occur when our Lord Jesus returns to the earth to begin His millennial reign. At that time Satan and all of his cohorts will be removed from the earth to be locked up in the bottomless pit. But I want you to notice that this passage also declares one of the reasons why Satan will be removed from the earth, i.e. so that he can no longer deceive the nations. So how does Satan deceive the nations of the world? He is able to deceive them because as the god of this world, he has blinded their minds to the truth, and more specifically to the truth of God's word. And so, just as Satan deceived Eve into believing that God's word was untrue and that she would not die when she ate the fruit of the knowledge of good and evil, even so Satan is able to deceive the nations of the world into believing that God's word is untrue while Satan's lies are the real truth.

To summarize; from our examination of the scriptures quoted in this section we have established numerous spiritual truths. We have established that Satan is indeed the god of this world, and how he became the god of this world. We have also established that Satan is a wicked ruler, intent on the destruction of mankind. We have mentioned the torment in hell which the devil and his angels know awaits them at the end of the age, which motivates them to take as many of mankind with them as possible. We have also established the limitations of Satan's authority in the earth, and how he deceives men into wilfully submitting themselves to his rule through the mechanism of sin. We have established that as the god of this world Satan only has authority over unbelievers and that he has no authority over the Lord's saints. And finally we have established that because Satan is the god of this

The church's adversary

world, he is therefore able to influence the behaviour of the whole world using the mechanism of deception. A whole book can be written exploring how, as the god of this world Satan reigns over the world, but that is not the subject of this book, for in this book we are specifically examining how the church is meant to deal with Satan in this world.

The church's adversary

1 Peter 5:8-9 "Be sober, be vigilant; because your adversary the devil walks about like a roaring lion, seeking whom he may devour. (9) Resist him, steadfast in the faith, knowing that the same sufferings are experienced by your brotherhood in the world."

In this section we want to discuss the biblical truth that Satan is the adversary of the church and what the ramifications of that truth are. We have already seen in the previous section that because Satan is the god of this world all unbelievers are therefore subject to his rule. It is important to note that because the spirit realm governs the natural realm, mankind is completely powerless to oppose the devil's rule in any way. Nevertheless there is a group of people in the earth today over which the devil has no authority, which is the church of our Lord Jesus Christ. It is precisely because believers are not subject to Satan's rule that they are the greatest threat to his reign in the earth. So why does the church pose such a threat to Satan's reign in the earth? The reason is because the church's mission is completely opposed to the devil's agenda, for whereas Satan and his angels are focused on

The church's adversary

destroying mankind, the church is focused on saving mankind. Therefore by default the church is working against the devil and his angels. And so Satan does everything in his power to destroy the church, which is why the above quoted passage of scripture refers to him as our adversary. In this passage the apostle Peter reveals a number of truths to us about our adversary, i.e. how he operates and how believers can deal with him. Peter opens his statement with an admonition for the saints to be sober and vigilant because the god of this world's agenda is the destruction of the saints. Peter goes on to teach us that Satan walks about like a roaring lion seeking whom he may devour. It is important to note that this passage declares that the devil seeks whom he "may" devour, thus implying that he can only devour those who choose not to resist him steadfast in the faith. Peter goes on in this passage to equate the devil's roaring to suffering experienced by the saints. And so we see that Satan's mode of operation against the saints is to initiate some form of suffering in the life of the believer to determine how they will react. As this passage declares, Satan has no recourse against the believer who chooses to resist him steadfast in the faith during their hour of trial. In other words he is unable to devour them. Obviously, for the believer who chooses not to resist him during their hour of trial the outcome will be very different.

Ephesians 6:10-13 "Finally, my brethren, be strong in the Lord and in the power of His might. (11) Put on the whole armour of God that you may be able to stand against the wiles of the devil. (12) For we do not wrestle against flesh and blood, but against principalities, against powers, against the rulers of the darkness of this age, against spiritual

The church's adversary

hosts of wickedness in the heavenly places. (13) Therefore, take up the whole armour of God that you may be able to withstand in the evil day, and having done all, to stand."

In the above quoted passage of scripture the apostle Paul gives us numerous insights into the church's ongoing conflict with the devil as the god of this world. In this passage Paul admonishes the believer to put on the whole armour of God. And so God would not instruct His saints to put on His armour if we were not at war. Clearly believers are at war, and this passage identifies the devil as our enemy and this world in which we live as the war zone. We see in this passage that although ultimately the believer's enemy is Satan himself, that the devil has a whole cohort of angels arrayed against us. For the scripture describes the various levels of angelic authorities that exist in Satan's kingdom, starting at the lowest level and ending with the highest level of authority in his kingdom i.e. principalities, powers, rulers of the darkness of this world and then finally spiritual hosts of wickedness in the heavenly places. It is important to note that no saint is excluded from this conflict, for this passage declares that all believers, not just a select few, are in a wrestling match against the devil and his angels. In this passage the Holy Spirit reveals two strategies that the devil uses against the believer in this conflict, for He mentions the wiles of the devil and the evil day. The wiles of the devil would be the various temptations that the devil places before the saint to try draw them aside from their walk of righteousness. And the evil day would be the sufferings that the apostle Peter spoke about earlier. In both instances the Holy Spirit counsels the saint to stand their ground and to give no place to the devil. Twice in this

The church's adversary

passage the apostle Paul admonishes the saints to put on the whole armour of God, thus emphasizing the fact that without God's armour the saints are no match for the devil and his angels.

> *Revelation 12:13-17 "Now when the dragon saw that he had been cast to the earth, he persecuted the woman who gave birth to the male Child. (14) But the woman was given two wings of a great eagle, that she might fly into the wilderness to her place, where she is nourished for a time and times and half a time, from the presence of the serpent. (15) So, the serpent spewed water out of his mouth like a flood after the woman that he might cause her to be carried away by the flood. (16) But the earth helped the woman, and the earth opened its mouth and swallowed up the flood which the dragon had spewed out of his mouth. (17) And the dragon was enraged with the woman, and he went to make war with the rest of her offspring, who keep the commandments of God and have the testimony of Jesus Christ."*

The above quoted passage of scripture describes an event that will take place at the end of the age, i.e. Satan attempting to destroy the nation of Israel when he and his angels are finally cast out of heaven. The woman in this passage represents the nation of Israel and the dragon represents the devil. This passage goes on to show us that because Satan's attempt to destroy Israel will prove to be unsuccessful at that time, that he will then turn his attention to waging war against those who have the testimony of Jesus Christ i.e. the church. And so this passage highlights two entities in the earth which the devil

The church's adversary

continually tries to destroy, i.e. Israel and the church. We have already discussed the reasons why Satan tries to destroy the church, but why does he also try to destroy the nation of Israel? Israel is unique because God has chosen that nation to fulfil His purposes in the earth. And so in an attempt to thwart God's purposes in the earth, Satan continuously tries to destroy the nation of Israel. Unlike the church however, Israel has no ability to resist the devil's actions and is not even aware of his actions against them. So how does Israel survive? I want you to notice that this passage declares that the earth helped the woman by opening its mouth to swallow the flood which spewed out of the dragon's mouth. And so we see that whenever the devil attempts to destroy her, in His sovereignty, God intervenes to protect the nation of Israel. Although this passage refers to a future event, it still confirms the truth that for different reasons, Satan continuously tries to destroy both the nation of Israel and the church. And so we see that Satan remains the adversary of the church.

To summarize; from our examination of the scriptures quoted in this section we have clearly established that the saints are in a war and that our war is against our adversary the devil and his angels. We also briefly mentioned the structure of Satan's angelic kingdom which is arrayed against the church. We have also discussed some of the mechanisms which Satan employs in his attempts to destroy the Lord's saints. We have established how vital it is for the saints to put on the full armour of God if they want to stand against the devil and his angels. We have established that not only does the devil attempt to destroy the church but that he also attempts to destroy the nation of Israel, and we discussed the reasons why he is determined to destroy both. We

The church's adversary

have also established that while the church has the ability to resist the devil for themselves, the nation of Israel has no such ability and thus the Lord in His sovereignty, protects them from the devil's attempts at their destruction.

Chapter 2
How Jesus destroyed the devil

The deceiver was deceived

Job 38:4-7 "Where were you when I laid the foundations of the earth? Tell Me, if you have understanding. (5) Who determined its measurements? Surely you know! Or who stretched the line upon it? (6) To what were its foundations fastened? Or who laid its cornerstone, (7) when the morning stars sang together, and all the sons of God shouted for joy?"

In the previous chapter we stated that Satan has no authority over the church, and so in this chapter we want to discuss how the Lord delivered us from the devil's authority. Therefore to begin with, in this section we want to discuss the biblical truth that Satan was deceived into believing that Jesus had committed sin and what the ramifications of that truth were. As we will see in this section it was vital for God to convince Satan that Jesus had committed sin, for unless God could do that His plan of salvation for mankind would never have succeeded. So why was it essential for Satan to be convinced that Jesus had sinned? In order for us to answer that question we need to go back to the beginning of creation. After God created all the angels it was at that point that He then created the earth. That truth is confirmed to us in the above quoted passage of scripture which is a record of

How Jesus destroyed the devil

God's discourse with Job, in which the Lord reveals that when He created the earth that all the angels of God shouted for joy, thus confirming to us that the angels were present when God created the earth. All the angels of God would have included Lucifer and his angels, for they were still a part of God's kingdom at that time. All of these events took place long before God created Adam and Eve.

> *Revelation 2:12-13 "And to the pastor of the church in Pergamos write, 'these things says He who has the sharp two-edged sword: (13) "I know your works, and where you dwell, where Satan's throne is. And you hold fast to My name, and did not deny My faith even in the days in which Antipas was My faithful martyr, who was killed among you, where Satan dwells."*

When God created the earth He placed it under Lucifer's dominion. Someone said but I thought God gave Adam dominion over the earth. In order for us to understand how it is possible for God to have given dominion over the earth to both Lucifer and Adam we first need to understand God's creation of the earth. Unlike the heavens which have only one dimension, God created the earth with two dimensions and both dimensions were created at the same time. And so whereas the heavens only exist in the realm of the spirit, the earth has both a spiritual and a physical realm and the two dimensions exist parallel to each other. Therefore God gave Lucifer dominion over the spiritual realm of the earth, while He gave Adam dominion over the physical realm of the earth. And so we see that because angels are celestial beings, Lucifer and his angels were given the spiritual dimension of the earth to dwell in, whereas

How Jesus destroyed the devil

because mankind are terrestrial beings, they were given the physical dimension of the earth to dwell in. God called both the spiritual and physical realms of the earth Eden, which is why the scripture states that God placed Adam in Eden the Garden of God (Genesis 2:15) and which is why God also described Lucifer as dwelling in Eden the garden of God (Ezekiel 28:13). When God gave Lucifer full dominion over all of spiritual earth He set up Lucifer's throne on the earth. That truth is confirmed to us in the account of Lucifer's rebellion against God, when he stated that he would ascend into heaven and exalt his throne above the angels of God (Isaiah 14:13). In the above quoted passage of scripture the Lord Jesus also confirmed this truth to us by mentioning that Satan's throne is located in the region of Pergamos. The fact that Satan still has his throne indicates that his dominion of spiritual earth has not yet ended. As an aside, obviously Satan's throne is not located in the region of Pergamos in the physical realm but rather in the parallel location in the spiritual realm.

Genesis 1:1-10 "In the beginning God created the heavens and the earth. (2) ... and darkness was on the face of the deep. And the Spirit of God was hovering over the face of the waters. ... (9) Then God said, "Let the waters under the heavens be gathered together into one place, and let the dry land appear"; and it was so. (10) And God called the dry land Earth, and the gathering together of the waters He called Seas. And God saw that it was good."

We have mentioned that God created the earth in two dimensions i.e. a spiritual realm and a physical realm, and the creation account in Genesis gives us some insight

How Jesus destroyed the devil

into how God did this. When God created the physical earth He covered it in water and darkness and left it in that state until the proper time came for it to be revealed. The reason God did that was because He created the physical dimension of the earth for men and not for angels, and the time for Adam to be created had not yet come. When the proper time did eventually arrive however, God then proceeded to reveal the physical earth, which is why God says in the above quoted passage of scripture "let the dry land appear". In other words the land was always there, it was just hidden under the water and darkness that had covered it from the beginning of creation.

> *Job 38:16-18 "Have you entered the springs of the sea? Or have you walked in search of the depths? (17) Have the gates of death been revealed to you? Or have you seen the doors of the shadow of death? (18) Have you comprehended the breadth of the earth? Tell Me, if you know all this."*

We have seen thus far that God created the earth with two dimensions i.e. a spiritual dimension and a physical dimension. We have also seen that God gave Lucifer dominion over the spiritual dimension of the earth. Scripture teaches us that the spiritual dimension of the earth is divided into three separate regions. The first region is located just above the earth, and is referred to as "the air" (Ephesians 2:2) or the first heaven (1 Corinthians 12:2). It is in this region that the angels with the highest level of authority in Satan's kingdom are located. The apostle Paul refers to these angels as spiritual hosts of wickedness in the heavenly places (Ephesians 6:12). The second region is located on the earth, and as we have

How Jesus destroyed the devil

already seen it is in this region that Satan's throne is located. It is also in this region that the angels with the second highest level of authority in Satan's kingdom are located i.e. the rulers of the darkness of this world. The third region is located under the earth, and for the purposes of this discussion it is this region which we want to explore. Scripture teaches us that this region is where Death is located (Revelation 6:8), which is why the Gates of Death are placed at its entrance. This region is then further sub divided into two separate regions, both of which are located beyond the Gates of Death. In the above quoted passage of scripture the Lord mentions these regions when He speaks about the Gates of Death and the depths. The depths that God speaks about in this passage refers to these two regions, the first of which our Lord Jesus called Abraham's bosom (Luke 16) or Paradise (Luke 23:43). God created this region as a place of comfort and rest for the saints when they died. The second region, which is located below Abraham's Bosom, has various names ascribed to it i.e. Hades, Sheol, Hell and the Bottomless Pit. Apollyon is the angel who rules over this region (Revelation 9:11). God created this region as a place of torment for the wicked when they die. Scripture teaches us that there is a great gulf fixed between the two regions, which prevented the occupants of either region from crossing over between them. And so we see that because Lucifer was given dominion over the regions under the earth that he was therefore given dominion over Death, Hades and Abraham's Bosom. So what happened when Lucifer rebelled against God? The answer to that question is that he transitioned from being and angel of light to become an angel of darkness and God changed his name to Satan and he was cast out of (the third) heaven (Luke 10:18). Because Lucifer's angels had

How Jesus destroyed the devil

joined him in his attempted rebellion (Revelation 12:4), they too transitioned from being angels of light to become angels of darkness, more commonly known as demons. Nevertheless what did not change is the dominion that God had given them, for scripture teaches us that the gifts and calling of God are irrevocable (Romans 11:29). And so whereas before it was Lucifer who had dominion over the regions under the earth, now it was Satan who had that exact same dominion. It is for this reason that scripture refers to Satan as having the power of death (Hebrews 2:14). The word translated "power" in that passage can also be translated "dominion", which is in fact a better translation in this passage; because it conveys to us the truth that Death fell under Satan's dominion. This is also the reason that Satan held the keys to Death and Hades (Revelation 1:18).

Romans 7:8-11 "But sin, taking opportunity by the commandment, produced in me all manner of evil desire. For apart from the law sin was dead. (9) I was alive once without the law, but when the commandment came, sin revived and I died. (10) And the commandment, which was to bring life, I found to bring death. (11) For sin, taking occasion by the commandment, deceived me, and by it killed me."

We have seen thus far that Death and Hades fell under Satan's domain. So the question is asked what impact did that have on mankind. In order for us to answer that question we first need to have an understanding of spiritual death and how it is incurred. Because their spirits come from God the Father of spirits (Hebrews 12:9), all men are born into the earth spiritually

How Jesus destroyed the devil

alive (John 1:9). For various reasons however, all men without exception, also commit sin (Romans 3:23). When men commit sin the first and immediate consequence is that they incur spiritual death (Romans 5:12). Adam and Eve found that out when they committed sin in the Garden of Eden, for God warned them that in the day they ate the forbidden fruit they would die, and that's exactly what happened (Genesis 2:16-17). And so we see that because of their sin all men, prior to the Lord Jesus going to the cross, were spiritually dead people. There was an exception however, for God deems children to have no knowledge of good and evil and therefore does not hold them accountable for sin (Deuteronomy 1:39), because of which they remain spiritually alive. Because God referred to the Lord Jesus as a child when He was twelve years old (Luke 2:42-43) we know therefore that thirteen is the age when God holds men accountable for sin for the first time. And so we see that because of their sin, at the age of thirteen all men die spiritually. In the above quoted passage of scripture the apostle Paul confirms this particular truth for us, for he describes the period in his life when he was a child and therefore spiritually alive, and how that changed on his thirteenth birthday when God held him accountable for his sin and as a consequence his spirit died. And so we see that because all men were dead in spirit they therefore fell under the domain of the one who had the power of death i.e. the devil. As an aside, this is the reason why Jesus taught us that we must be born again, because we need to be made spiritually alive once again.

Isaiah 14:12-17 "How you are fallen from heaven, O Lucifer, son of the morning! How you are cut down to the ground, you who weakened the

How Jesus destroyed the devil

nations! (13) For you have said in your heart: 'I will ascend into heaven, I will exalt my throne above the stars of God; I will also sit on the mount of the congregation On the farthest sides of the north; (14) I will ascend above the heights of the clouds, I will be like the Most High.' (15) Yet you shall be brought down to Sheol, to the lowest depths of the Pit. (16) "Those who see you will gaze at you, And consider you, saying: 'Is this the man who made the earth tremble, Who shook kingdoms, (17) Who made the world as a wilderness And destroyed its cities, Who did not open the house of his prisoners?'"

We have seen thus far that because Death and Hades fell under Satan's domain, all men who were spiritually dead were therefore subject to his authority. So how did that truth affect mankind? In the above quoted passage of scripture the Holy Spirit answers that question by telling us that Satan did not open the house of his prisoners. So what does that statement mean? As we have already mentioned, prior to the Lord Jesus going to the cross, all of mankind were spiritually dead people, saints and wicked alike (Luke 9:60), because of which they all fell under the authority of the one who held the power of death, which is the devil. And so when their time on the earth expired, all of mankind were taken down into the lower parts of the earth to enter through the Gates of Death into the region of Death. The only difference between the saints and the wicked at that time was that once taken through the gates of death they were separated; the saints being taken to Abraham's bosom while the wicked were taken into Hades. Nevertheless even though the saints were held in a place of comfort and rest, they were still being held as prisoners by Satan who

How Jesus destroyed the devil

had the power of death. And so we see that because the saints at that time were spiritually dead people and had not yet been born again i.e. made spiritually alive once again, they could not yet ascend into heaven. As an aside, it is important to note that children, from conception to the age of thirteen, are still spiritually alive and do not therefore fall under Satan's authority. And so when children die they are not taken down into the lower parts of the earth, but rather they are taken up into heaven to be with God.

Hebrews 2:14-15 "Inasmuch then as the children have partaken of flesh and blood, He Himself likewise shared in the same, that through death He might destroy him who had the power of death, that is, the devil, (15) and release those who through fear of death were all their lifetime subject to bondage."

And so we see that because he had the power of death, that after their time on earth had expired, Satan had the legal right to hold prisoner in the regions of death, all who were spiritually dead. Scripture teaches us that God is the God of the living and not the dead (Mark 12:27), and so He had no authority to act on the saints behalf, because He had given that authority to the devil. And so the only way God could solve this problem was to deal with the one who had the power of death i.e. the devil. In the above quoted passage of scripture the Holy Spirit gives us some insight into how God did this, for it states that the Lord Jesus destroyed the Devil who had the power of death. This passage goes on to declare that once the devil was destroyed that those who had been subject to his bondage could then be released. So how did the

How Jesus destroyed the devil

Lord Jesus destroy the devil? He couldn't just walk into Satan's domain and destroy him, because that would have violated the authority which Satan had received from God; something which was impossible for Jesus to do. And so this passage teaches us that it was through death itself that Jesus was able to destroy the devil. In other words in order for Jesus to legally destroy the devil Jesus had to die, but more specifically God had to ensure that Satan was the one who killed His Son. So why was that so important? Because Jesus had never committed any sin, Satan would have acted unlawfully if he killed the Lord and took Him down into Hades to suffer torment. And so we see that whereas Jesus couldn't violate Satan's authority by walking into his domain to destroy him, God ensured that Satan violated his own authority by committing the unlawful act of killing Jesus and taking Him down into Hades to suffer torment, thus opening the door for the Son of God to destroy the devil in his own domain.

> *Ephesians 5:8 "For you were once darkness, but now you are light in the Lord. Walk as children of light."*

We have stated thus far that in order for Jesus to be able to destroy the devil, God had to persuade him to kill Jesus and take Him down into Hades to suffer torment. So how did God do that? In order to do that God had to convince Satan that Jesus had become subject to his authority. As we have already seen, it is only those who have died spiritually as a result of their sin that fall under Satan's authority. And so we see that God had to convince Satan that Jesus had died spiritually as a result of sin that He had committed. So how did God do that? When men

How Jesus destroyed the devil

incur spiritual death their spirits transition from light to darkness. We saw that same phenomenon occur when Satan and his angels rebelled against God, for they transitioned from being angels of light to become angels of darkness. The apostle Paul confirms that truth for us in the above quoted passage of scripture by describing the spiritual condition of saints before and after they are saved, for he declares that before we were saved that we were darkness, but now we are light in the Lord. It is the spirit of the individual that is either light or darkness. In other words if God were to allow us to see into the spirit realm we would see that the spirits of the saved are light while the spirits of the unsaved are darkness. Therefore because Satan resides in the spirit realm he sees the condition of the spirits of men, thus identifying who is subject to him and who isn't. And so in order for God to convince the devil that Jesus had become subject to his authority, God had to ensure that Jesus' spirit transitioned from light to darkness, which could only happen if Jesus had died in spirit as a result of sin.

2 Corinthians 5:21 "For He made Him who knew no sin to be sin for us, that we might become the righteousness of God in Him."

When Jesus was born into the earth the devil understood that He was sent to execute God's plan of salvation for mankind, although at that time the devil had no idea what that plan was. And so in his attempt to thwart God's plan Satan had two options available; he could either kill Jesus or tempt Him to commit sin, and so he chose to employ both options. The first option which we will discuss is Satan's attempt to kill Jesus. So why would Satan try to kill Jesus? Satan knew that Jesus was

How Jesus destroyed the devil

not immortal, because as we read earlier Jesus had the same body that all men have i.e. a body made of flesh and blood. In other words Jesus' body was mortal just as all men are. And so Satan knew that if Jesus died while He was spiritually alive that, just like all children who die, He would ascend back into heaven to be with God. In other words as one that was not spiritually dead Jesus would be unable to descend into Satan's domain of death, and thus He would be precluded from implementing God's plan of salvation. And so on numerous occasions Satan attempted to have the Lord Jesus killed. For example Herod tried to kill Him when He was a baby, His hometown of Nazareth tried to throw Him off a cliff and on numerous occasions the Jews tried to stone Him. However, as long as Jesus remained spiritually alive, all of Satan's attempts to kill Jesus proved to be unsuccessful because God protected Him. This brings us to the second option which Satan employed, which was his attempt to tempt the Lord Jesus to commit sin. It is obvious why Satan would use this option, because if it proved to be successful then Jesus would incur the penalty of sin i.e. He would die in spirit and thus fall under Satan's authority as the one who had the power of death, and thus Satan would have thwarted God's plan of salvation. And so on numerous occasions Satan attempted to tempt the Lord Jesus to commit sin. For example Jesus successfully overcame all three of Satan's attempts to tempt Him in the wilderness. Nevertheless even though Satan was unsuccessful on that occasion, scripture teaches us that the devil departed from Jesus until an opportune time (Luke 4:13). In other words there were other occasions when the devil tempted the Lord. Nevertheless all of Satan's attempts to tempt the Lord Jesus proved to be unsuccessful because the Lord never committed any sin; until the time arrived for God's

How Jesus destroyed the devil

plan of salvation to be made manifest. We have seen that Satan's attempts to kill the Lord Jesus and his attempts to tempt Him to commit sin all proved to be unsuccessful. So how did God accomplish that which Satan had found impossible to do? The answer lies in the above quoted passage of scripture, for this passage declares that God made Jesus who knew no sin to be sin for us. So what does that statement mean? It means that God took the sin of the world and placed it on His Son. The moment God did that, Jesus' spirit incurred the punishment of sin i.e. His spirit died and Jesus became subject to the one who had the power of death, i.e. the devil. Although this passage reveals to us how God made His Son to be sin, it does not reveal how God was able to convince the devil that Jesus had finally committed sin. So why was that so important? If God had simply made Jesus to become sin with our sin, Satan and his angels would have immediately suspected that something was not right, because they had first hand experience as to just how impervious Jesus was to committing sin. And so if Satan and his angels suspected anything untoward they would never have killed Jesus, thus denying Him access to their domain of death.

Luke 22:2-6 "And the chief priests and the scribes sought how they might kill Him, for they feared the people. (3) Then Satan entered Judas, surnamed Iscariot, who was numbered among the twelve. (4) So he went his way and conferred with the chief priests and captains, how he might betray Him to them. (5) And they were glad, and agreed to give him money. (6) So he promised and sought opportunity to betray Him to them in the absence of the multitude."

How Jesus destroyed the devil

So how did God convince the devil that Jesus had finally committed sin? The answer lies in the above quoted passage of scripture, for in this passage we see that Satan himself influenced Judas to betray Jesus. This action which Satan took raises two questions; firstly, why was Satan interested in influencing Judas to betray the Lord Jesus, and secondly, why had Satan specifically chosen Judas for that task? To answer both questions we first need to discuss how the Lord Jesus appointed His twelve apostles. Scripture teaches us that prior to the Lord choosing His apostles that He spent all night in prayer to God, and the following morning He called His disciples to Himself; and from them He then chose twelve whom He named apostles, of whom Judas was one (Luke 6:12-16). And so, for the devil who was observing our Lord's actions, it looked like the Lord spent all night in prayer to make sure that He chose correctly i.e. those whom God had preordained to be His twelve apostles. But if we examine scripture more closely we see that right from the outset Jesus knew exactly who His twelve apostles were, and not only that but Jesus also knew that Judas had been chosen to betray Him (John 6:64-71). And so we see that the Lord's actions on the night prior to His appointing of the twelve were designed to create an illusion to convince the devil that Jesus was prayerfully seeking God's counsel, because He couldn't afford to make a mistake in His choosing of the twelve apostles. God needed to create that illusion to reinforce the devil's suspicion. So what did Satan suspect? In observing the Lord's twelve apostles the devil knew that Judas was a thief and that he was stealing from the Lord's ministry finances (John 12:6). And so Satan became convinced that Jesus had missed God in choosing Judas, for Satan could not conceive that God

How Jesus destroyed the devil

would have chosen a thief to be one of the twelve apostles of the Lamb. Therefore it was for this reason that Satan was so keen to persuade Judas to betray the Lord Jesus, for he reasoned that if he could persuade Judas to betray Jesus, it would prove that Jesus had disobeyed God in choosing him. In other words Jesus would have committed sin. And so we see that when Judas betrayed the Lord Jesus with a kiss on the night before the Lord was crucified (Luke 22:48) that it was in that moment that God placed the sin of the world on His Son. The moment that happened, Satan saw the Lord's spirit transition from light to darkness as He incurred spiritual death. And so Satan was deceived into thinking that Jesus had committed sin by appointing Judas whom God had not chosen. And because Satan was convinced that Jesus had indeed committed sin resulting in Jesus incurring spiritual death, he was also convinced that Jesus now fell under his authority as the one who had the power of death. And so we see that Judas' betrayal of the Lord Jesus played a crucial role in God's plan of salvation.

To summarize; from our examination of the scriptures quoted in this section we have seen that the angels were present when God created the earth, and that God created the earth with two dimensions i.e. a physical and a spiritual dimension. We have also seen that God gave Lucifer dominion over the spiritual dimension of the earth, which included the spiritual regions under the earth. We have seen that when Lucifer transitioned into Satan that he retained his dominion over the spiritual regions under the earth, which included the Gates of Death, Paradise and Hades. We have also seen that, because of their sin, all men incur spiritual death at the age of thirteen and therefore fall under the authority of the one who has the power of death i.e. the devil. We have

How Jesus destroyed the devil

seen that because all men fall under Satan's authority, that when they die they all descend into the region of death where they are held captive either in Paradise or in Hades. We have also seen that in order for God to be able to release Satan's prisoners that Jesus had to be killed by the devil. We have seen that Satan had to become convinced that Jesus committed sin and how God accomplished that. We then saw how through the betrayal of Judas Iscariot that God was able to convince the devil that Jesus had finally fallen under his authority.

Satan killed Jesus

1 Corinthians 2:7-8 "But we speak the wisdom of God in a mystery, the hidden wisdom which God ordained before the ages for our glory, (8) which none of the rulers of this age knew; for had they known, they would not have crucified the Lord of glory."

In this section we want to discuss why the devil had to kill Jesus in order for God's plan of salvation to work. The above quoted passage of scripture reveals to us that God had ordained the salvation of mankind before the ages. In other words God had ordained His plan of salvation even before Lucifer and his angels were created. Nevertheless God's plan of salvation remained hidden from everyone, including Satan and his angels, for this passage teaches us that if Satan and his angels had known what God was doing through the death of His Son Jesus, they would never have crucified the Lord of glory. So the question is asked, why Satan and his angels would have refused to crucify Jesus if they had known what God was

How Jesus destroyed the devil

doing. We have seen in the previous section that from the moment that Jesus was born into the earth that Satan tried to kill Him. For you will recall that Herod tried to have Him killed when He was born in the town of Bethlehem and Joseph was warned by God in a dream to take Jesus down into Egypt (Matthew 2:13). Satan also tried on numerous occasions to kill Jesus during His earthly ministry, for in His home town of Nazareth they tried to throw Him off a cliff (Luke 4:29), and on more than one occasion the Jews tried to stone Him (John 8:59), and then the Chief priests and the Pharisees also plotted to put Him to death (John 11:53). Satan was the instigator behind all of those attempts to kill the Lord Jesus. We have seen in the previous section that the reason why Satan was so intent on killing Jesus was because he recognised that if Jesus died while He was spiritually alive, Jesus would have been forced to ascend back into heaven and would have thus been precluded from descending into Satan's domain of the region of death. Nevertheless all of Satan's attempts to kill the Lord Jesus failed, and the reason for that was because Jesus' time had not yet come (John 8:20). So why was the Lord's crucifixion different? It was different because God could only allow His Son to be killed after Jesus was made to be sin, so that as one who had therefore incurred spiritual death He would be taken down into hell, which was the domain over which Satan had control. We have seen in the previous section that God had given Satan the power of Death and Hades. And so in order for God to be able to legally take that authority back from Satan, He had to manipulate Satan into killing His Son Jesus and take Him into hell to suffer torment. And so as this passage declares, had Satan and his angels understood what God

How Jesus destroyed the devil

was doing they would never have crucified the Lord Jesus, thus preventing Him from gaining access to their domain.

> *Hebrews 2:9-15 "But we see Jesus, who was made a little lower than the angels, for the suffering of death crowned with glory and honour, that He, by the grace of God, might taste death for everyone. (10) For it was fitting for Him, for whom are all things and by whom are all things, in bringing many sons to glory, to make the captain of their salvation perfect through sufferings. (11) For both He who sanctifies and those who are being sanctified are all of one, for which reason He is not ashamed to call them brethren, (12) saying: "I will declare Your name to my brethren; in the midst of the assembly I will sing praise to You." (13) And again: "I will put my trust in Him." And again: "Here am I and the children whom God has given me." (14) Inasmuch then as the children have partaken of flesh and blood, He Himself likewise shared in the same, that through death He might destroy him who had the power of death, that is, the devil, (15) and release those who through fear of death were all their lifetime subject to bondage."*

In the above quoted passage of scripture the Holy Spirit teaches us that there was a time when Jesus was made a little lower than the angels. This statement poses two questions; why would God allow His Son to be made lower than the angels and when did that happen? It was certainly not when Jesus walked in the flesh that He was made lower than Satan and his angels, or even God's angels for that matter. We know that, because Satan and his angels were fully subjected to the Lord's authority

How Jesus destroyed the devil

during that time (Luke 10:17-19). And as far as God's angels were concerned, Jesus Himself stated that He could command them any time He chose (Matthew 26:53). This passage of scripture explains exactly when and the reason why Jesus was made a little lower than the angels, for we see that it was for the suffering of death that Jesus was made lower than the angels. We have already seen in the previous chapter that all who are spiritually dead fall under Satan's authority. And so we see that it was when Jesus was made to be sin and died in spirit, that He was made lower than Satan and his angels who, because they had the power of death, were therefore able to exercise their authority over Him. It was precisely because Jesus now fell under Satan's authority that Satan then proceeded to crucify Him. We know that Jesus had been delivered to Satan's authority during that time and we know that Satan was the one who instigated the Lord's crucifixion, because Jesus said that Satan had the greater sin for delivering Him to Pilot to be crucified (John 19:10-11). The above quoted passage of scripture goes on to teach us that it was through death that Jesus was able to destroy the one who had the power of death (the devil) and set his captives free. In other words the only way that Jesus could gain access to Satan's domain was through death, which is why God had to persuade Satan and his angels to kill the Lord Jesus. And so we see that it was because Satan and his angels were deceived into thinking that they finally had authority over the Son of God that they then proceeded to crucify Him.

To summarize; from our examination of the scriptures quoted in this section we have seen that God's plan of salvation was prepared before Lucifer and his angels were created. We have seen that God's plan of salvation was hidden from Satan and his angels, for had

How Jesus destroyed the devil

they known what God was doing they would have refused to kill the Lord Jesus. We have seen the importance of the timing of the death of Jesus i.e. it could only take place after God had made Him to be sin. We have also seen that God had to persuade the devil that he had the authority to kill His Son and that God did that by allowing His Son to incur the penalty of sin i.e. spiritual death.

Why Jesus went to Hades

Matthew 12:39-40 "But He answered and said to them, "An evil and adulterous generation seeks after a sign, and no sign will be given to it except the sign of the prophet Jonah. (40) For as Jonah was three days and three nights in the belly of the great fish, so will the Son of Man be three days and three nights in the heart of the earth."

In this section we want to discuss the two reasons why, after His death on the cross, the Lord Jesus was taken into Hell. In the above quoted passage of scripture the Lord Jesus confirmed to us that after His death He would be taken into the heart of the earth for three days and three nights. We have already established that the region of Death is located in the heart of the earth and that Satan has dominion over that region. We have also established that the region of death is further subdivided into two separate regions i.e. Paradise and Hades. And so the Lord's statement raises the question as to which region of death Jesus was taken to?

Acts 2:25-28 "For David says concerning Him: 'I foresaw the Lord always before My face, for He is

How Jesus destroyed the devil

at My right hand, that I may not be shaken. (26) Therefore My heart rejoiced, and My tongue was glad; moreover My flesh also will rest in hope. (27) For you will not leave My soul in Hades, nor will You allow Your Holy One to see corruption. (28) You have made known to Me the ways of life; You will make Me full of joy in Your presence."

    The above quoted passage of scripture answers the question we have asked, i.e. which part of the region of death was the Lord Jesus taken to; for in this passage the Lord plainly tells us that He was taken to Hades while His body lay in the tomb. This passage not only reveals to us that Jesus was taken into Hades however, but it also gives us further insight into why our Lord went there in the first place, and why He was there for three days and three nights. Firstly we see that the reason why Jesus was taken to Hades was because God had decreed that He should be taken there, and we also see that God was the one who would bring Him out from there; for in this passage Jesus stated that God would not leave His soul in Hades. Secondly we see that one of the reasons why Jesus went into Hades for three days and three nights was because God would not allow His body to see corruption. Under normal circumstances the human body begins to decay three days after death, and so we see that Jesus had to be raised from the dead after three days in order to prevent His body from experiencing any decay.

    Psalms 71:10-11 "For my enemies speak against me; and those who lie in wait for my life take counsel together, (11) Saying, "God has forsaken him; Pursue and take him, for there is none to deliver him."

How Jesus destroyed the devil

We have seen thus far that it was God who had decreed that Jesus was to be taken down into Hades after His death. Obviously it was the devil that carried out God's decree, for he was the one who had the power of death and who held the keys of Hades. In the above quoted passage of scripture we see that after Jesus incurred spiritual death that God had forsaken Him, for you will recall the words of the Lord Jesus when He hung on the cross, "My God, My God, why have You forsaken Me?" (Mark 15:34). And so realising that God had forsaken Jesus and that there was therefore none who could deliver Him from their dominion, Satan and his angels then proceeded to kill Jesus and take Him down into Hades.

2 Samuel 22:5-18 *"When the waves of death surrounded me, the floods of ungodliness made me troubled. (6) The sorrows of Sheol surrounded me; the snares of death confronted me. ... (17) "He sent from above, He took me, He drew me out of many waters. (18) He delivered me from my strong enemy, from those who hated me; for they were too strong for me."*

The above quoted passage of scripture gives us a brief glimpse into what it was like for Jesus when He was taken down into Sheol. The point that I want to emphasize from this passage however, is that Jesus stated that the devil and his angels were too strong for Him, because of which He was powerless to prevent them from taking Him down into Hades. And so this passage confirms the truth that Jesus had been made lower than the devil and his angels during that time.

How Jesus destroyed the devil

Psalms 88:4-7 "I am counted with those who go down to the pit; I am like a man who has no strength, (5) Adrift among the dead, Like the slain who lie in the grave, Whom You remember no more, and who are cut off from Your hand. (6) You have laid me in the lowest pit, in darkness, in the depths. (7) Your wrath lies heavy upon me, and You have afflicted me with all Your waves."

So why did God decree that His Son should be taken down into Hades after His death on the cross? As I have already mentioned, there were two reasons why God did that. The first reason was because, prior to the death of Jesus, God had placed the sin of the whole world on His Son, and that sin had to be dealt with. In other words Jesus had to incur the punishment for those sins. And so we see in the above quoted passage of scripture, that God placed Jesus in the lowest pit of Hell where He incurred the wrath of God for the sins of the world. It is important to note that throughout this time Satan and his angels were fully convinced that Jesus was incurring the wrath of God for His own sin i.e. His sin of disobedience. After three days and three nights however, Jesus had fully paid the price for all of the sin of the world, which is why the apostle Paul teaches us that Jesus was delivered up because of our offences and was raised up because of our justification (Romans 4:25). And so it was that on the third day, when God's justice had been fully satisfied and all of the sins of the world had been fully paid for, that God could then reveal the second reason why He had allowed the devil and his angels to take Jesus into Hades.

How Jesus destroyed the devil

Colossians 1:18 "And he is the head of the body, the church: who is the beginning, the firstborn from the dead; that in all things he might have the pre-eminence."

As we have already mentioned, Satan and his angels had no idea what was really going on, i.e. that Jesus Himself had not sinned and that He was in fact incurring the wrath of God for the sins of the world. And so they fully expected Jesus to be held captive in their domain for all eternity, suffering the eternal wrath of God. Their delusion was shattered on the third day however, when Jesus was made alive once again. In the above quoted passage of scripture the apostle Paul teaches us that Jesus was the firstborn from the dead. It is interesting to note that scripture does not refer to Jesus as being the first to be raised from the dead, but it does refer to Him as being the firstborn from the dead. So what is the difference? To be raised from the dead refers to one's physical body being made alive once again. And so scripture could not refer to Jesus as being the first raised from the dead because there had been numerous incidents of people being raised from the dead before Jesus was. For example, there were three people who were raised from the dead in the Old Testament and Jesus Himself had raised three people from the dead when He walked on the earth. To be born from the dead however, refers to one's spirit being made alive once again. And so we see that every saint that is born again is born from the dead, for we were all once dead in trespasses and sins and God has made us alive in spirit once again (Ephesians 2:1). Nevertheless the first one, who was made alive in spirit once again i.e. born from the dead, was the Lord Jesus Christ.

How Jesus destroyed the devil

Psalms 18:16-42 "He sent from above, He took me; He drew me out of many waters. (17) He delivered me from my strong enemy, from those who hated me, for they were too strong for me. (18) They confronted me in the day of my calamity, but the Lord was my support. (19) He also brought me out into a broad place; He delivered me because He delighted in me. (20) The Lord rewarded me according to my righteousness; According to the cleanness of my hands He has recompensed me. (21) For I have kept the ways of the Lord and have not wickedly departed from my God. (22) For all His judgments were before me, and I did not put away His statutes from me. (23) I was also blameless before Him, and I kept myself from my iniquity. (24) Therefore, the Lord has recompensed me according to my righteousness, According to the cleanness of my hands in His sight. (25) With the merciful You will show Yourself merciful; With a blameless man You will show Yourself blameless; (26) With the pure You will show Yourself pure; And with the devious You will show Yourself shrewd. (27) For You will save the humble people but will bring down haughty looks. (28) For You will light my lamp; The Lord my God will enlighten my darkness. (29) For by You I can run against a troop, by my God I can leap over a wall. (30) As for God, His way is perfect; the word of the Lord is proven; He is a shield to all who trust in Him. (31) For who is God, except the Lord? And who is a rock, except our God? (32) It is God who arms me with strength and makes my way perfect. (33) He makes my feet like the feet of deer and sets me on my high places. (34) He teaches my hands to make war, so that my arms can bend a bow

How Jesus destroyed the devil

of bronze. (35) You have also given me the shield of Your salvation; Your right hand has held me up, Your gentleness has made me great. (36) You enlarged my path under me, so my feet did not slip. (37) I have pursued my enemies and overtaken them; neither did I turn back again till they were destroyed. (38) I have wounded them, so that they could not rise; they have fallen under my feet. (39) For You have armed me with strength for the battle; You have subdued under me those who rose up against me. (40) You have also given me the necks of my enemies, so that I destroyed those who hated me. (41) They cried out, but there was none to save; even to the Lord, but He did not answer them. (42) Then I beat them as fine as the dust before the wind; I cast them out like dirt in the streets."

  The above quoted passage of scripture is a vivid account of what transpired when God made Jesus alive on the third day. This was an event which took Satan and his angels by complete surprise because in their minds such an action was impossible, for God Himself had decreed that all who were spiritually dead were placed under the dominion of the one who had the power of death i.e. the devil. So how could God override Satan's authority by making Jesus alive in spirit once again? God could do this because, as our Lord stated in this passage, God recompensed Jesus according to His righteousness. So what does that statement mean? It means that because Jesus had never committed any sin Himself, spiritual death had no legal dominion over Him. And so God could legally make Jesus spiritually alive once again, i.e. God recompensed Jesus according to His righteousness. You will recall that we have stated that because Jesus had no

How Jesus destroyed the devil

legal way of accessing Satan's domain to strip him of his authority, God had to persuade Satan of his own accord to kill the Lord Jesus and take Him down into the region of death, which is exactly what happened. Of God's creations there is none more devious than the devil; nevertheless the shrewdness of God far surpasses the devil's deviousness. And so we see that Satan the deceiver was completely deceived, which is why the Lord Jesus tells us in this passage that with the devious God shows Himself shrewd. For although Satan and his angels thought they had defeated God's purpose through the killing of His Son, they were in fact acting as God had always intended they should; so that His purpose of eternal redemption could be accomplished. And so the moment Jesus was once again made alive in spirit He was no longer subject to Satan's dominion. In other words He was no longer lower than the devil and his angels, which meant that Jesus could once again use His power to deal with them. This passage reveals to us that Satan and his angels fled when they saw what was happening and that Jesus pursued them and overtook them. Jesus then proceeded to beat them until they lay wounded and helpless on the ground before Him. As a sign of His total dominance over them, Jesus then proceeded to place His foot on the back of the necks of Satan and his angels, which is the same thing that Joshua and his generals did to the kings of the nations which they defeated in battle (Joshua 10:24). Because Satan and his angels had been completely deceived they honestly believed that Jesus was acting illegally, for this passage declares that they even cried out to God for help but God did not answer them. The reason that God did not answer them was because Jesus was fulfilling that which God the Father had always predestined would take place.

How Jesus destroyed the devil

Colossians 2:13-15 "And you, being dead in your trespasses and the uncircumcision of your flesh, He has made alive together with Him, having forgiven you all trespasses, (14) having wiped out the handwriting of requirements that was against us, which was contrary to us. And He has taken it out of the way, having nailed it to the cross. (15) Having disarmed principalities and powers, He made a public spectacle of them, triumphing over them in it."

In the above quoted passage of scripture the apostle Paul confirms to us what to took place on the third day, for Paul tells us that not only did Jesus disarm principalities and powers, but He also made a public spectacle of them as He triumphed over them. In other words not only did Jesus completely destroy Satan along with his ruling angels, He also did it in full view of Satan's entire realm thus completely humiliating them. The word translated "disarm" in this passage can also be translated "spoil". To despoil someone means to forcefully strip that person of something of value. And so we see that after Jesus destroyed the devil and his angels He then proceeded to strip them of their God given authority. Jesus could legally do that now, because the devil and his angels had abused their authority when they killed Him and took Him down into the lower parts of Hell.

Revelation 1:18 "I am He who lives, and was dead, and behold, I am alive forevermore. Amen. And I have the keys of Hades and of Death."

How Jesus destroyed the devil

So what item or items of value did Jesus strip from the devil after He destroyed him? Jesus answers that question for us in the above quoted passage of scripture, for He tells us in this passage that He now holds the keys of Hades and of Death. Before the Lord's crucifixion the devil had held the keys of Hades and of Death, for God had placed those realms under Satan's authority. And so we see that Jesus took the keys of Hades and of Death from Satan thus striping him of his authority over those realms. It is for this reason that Jesus is now Lord of both the living and the dead (Romans 14:9). It is important to note that all which we have discussed in this section took place in the heart of the earth. In other words it took place before the Lord Jesus ascended to the tomb, entered His physical body and was physically raised from the dead.

To summarize; from our examination of the scriptures quoted in this section we have seen that after His death on the cross, that the Lord Jesus was taken down into Hades for three days and three nights. We have seen that not only were Satan and his angels responsible for killing Jesus, but they were also responsible for taking Jesus into the lowest pit of hell where He suffered torment. We have seen that the reason the devil and his angels could do what they did, was because for that brief moment in time Jesus had been made lower than them i.e. He was subject to their authority. We saw that the first reason why Jesus had to be taken down into Hell was to incur God's wrath, i.e. He had to pay the price for the sins of the world. We have seen that once God's justice had been fully satisfied that God could legally make His Son alive in spirit once again, i.e. Jesus became the firstborn from the dead. We have seen that when that happened that the second reason why Jesus had to be taken down into hell was revealed; because Jesus now had the legal

How Jesus destroyed the devil

right to destroy the devil and his angels. We have also seen that because Satan and his angels were completely deceived by God's plan of redemption, they were powerless to resist the Lord Jesus as He proceeded to destroy them, making a public spectacle of them in the process. We then saw that Jesus stripped the devil of his authority by taking the keys of Hades and Death from him, and that Jesus holds those keys today.

Jesus' authority

Matthew 28:18 "And Jesus came and spoke to them, saying, "All authority has been given to Me in heaven and on earth."

In this section we want to discuss firstly what level of authority has been given to Jesus after His death on the cross, and secondly how He is using that authority today? In answer to our first question, the Lord Jesus in the above quoted passage of scripture declares that He has been given all authority; both in heaven and on earth. In other words all of God's creation is now subject to the Lordship of Jesus. There are two further points that are clearly implied in this passage. Firstly, God Himself is the one who has given all authority to the Lord Jesus. And secondly, it is clear that Jesus received that authority only after His death, burial and resurrection. In other words He did not have that level of authority before He went to the cross.

Philippians 2:8-11 "And being found in appearance as a man, He humbled Himself and became obedient to the point of death, even the death

How Jesus destroyed the devil

of the cross. (9) Therefore, God also has highly exalted Him and given Him the name which is above every name, (10) that at the name of Jesus every knee should bow, of those in heaven, and of those on earth, and of those under the earth, (11) and that every tongue should confess that Jesus Christ is Lord, to the glory of God the Father."

In the above quoted passage of scripture the apostle Paul confirms to us that as a result of the finished work of the cross, that God has given Jesus the name which is above every name. In other words, other than God the Father, there is no one in all of God's creation that is not subject to the Lordship of Jesus, for this passage declares that God has decreed that every tongue must confess that Jesus Christ is Lord. It is important to note that Paul includes all three realms of God's creation in this passage, i.e. heaven, earth and the realms under the earth. Prior to the Lord Jesus going to the cross, the realms under the earth fell under Satan's domain; but that has since changed and Jesus is now Lord of all three realms, i.e. heaven, earth and the realms under the earth.

Ephesians 4:8-10 "Therefore He says: "when He ascended on high, He led captivity captive, and gave gifts to men." (9) (Now this, "He ascended"-- what does it mean but that He also first descended into the lower parts of the earth? (10) He who descended is also the One who ascended far above all the heavens, that He might fill all things.)"

We have seen earlier that before Jesus went to the cross, Satan held the keys of Hades and of Death, because of which all of mankind were held captive by him in death.

How Jesus destroyed the devil

And so in order to set mankind free Jesus gave His life as a ransom for us all (1 Timothy 2:6), for the purpose of a ransom being paid is to release those who are being held captive. The passage of scripture quoted above teaches us that when Jesus ascended into heaven that He led captivity captive. So what does that statement mean? As we have already seen, even though the Old Testament saints were kept separate from the unbelievers in death, nevertheless they were still held captive by Satan who had the keys of Death. And so the apostle Peter teaches us that after Jesus was raised from the dead that He went into Abraham's bosom to preach the gospel to the Old Testament saints; so that they could believe and thus be born again (1 Peter 3:19). It is those saints that Jesus then led with Him into heaven; and the reason Jesus could do that was because He now held the keys of Hades and of Death. And so we see that one of the first acts of Jesus using His newly acquired authority was to release the Old Testament saints from their captivity of death.

> *Hebrews 2:8 "You have put all things in subjection under His feet." For in that He put all in subjection under him, He left nothing that is not put under him. But now we do not yet see all things put under him."*

The question is asked, if all authority has been given to the Lord Jesus then why hasn't He done away with Satan and his angels and set up His reign in the earth? The answer to that question is twofold. Firstly, the end of the age has not yet come, because of which Jesus cannot yet remove Satan and his angels from the earth (Matthew 8:29). Secondly, even though Jesus has been given authority over all of God's creation, nevertheless for

How Jesus destroyed the devil

the present moment He has deliberately limited the exercising of His authority in the earth. In confirmation of that concept, the above quoted passage of scripture teaches us that even though God the Father has made all of creation subject to His Son, we do not yet see all things put under Him. So the question is asked, who is not yet subject to the Lordship of Jesus? The answer to that question is all of mankind living on the earth, both believer and unbeliever alike. The reason for that is because both believers and unbelievers have a free will, and in this life God will not allow the free will of mankind to be overridden. With regards to believers in the earth, they are required to willingly submit themselves to the Lordship of Jesus. Nevertheless even believers can choose to walk in the flesh in certain areas of their lives, and therefore not walk in full submission to the Lordship of Jesus. When believers leave this life however, their flesh is done away with and with their spirits they gladly submit themselves fully to His Lordship. With regards to unbelievers in the earth, they are required to willingly submit themselves to the Lordship of Jesus by confessing Him as Lord so that they can be saved. Nevertheless unbelievers choose rather to walk according to their own sinful lusts and therefore reject the Lordship of Jesus. When unbelievers leave this life however, they are forced to submit to the Lordship of Jesus as, against their wills, they are cast into hell. The status quo of the free will of men on the earth will remain in place until the end of the age, at which point we will see Satan and his angles removed from the earth and all of mankind will then become subject to the Lordship of Jesus. And so in answer to our second question which we asked at the beginning of this section i.e. how is Jesus using His authority today; we see that Jesus has begun to enforce His authority in the

How Jesus destroyed the devil

realms under the earth i.e. He has emptied Abraham's bosom. Nevertheless Jesus has not yet begun to enforce His authority over mankind living on the earth.

To summarize; from our examination of the scriptures quoted in this section we have seen that after His resurrection, that God the Father has given all authority to Jesus the Son of Man, which He clearly never had before. We have seen that Jesus has been given authority over all three of God's created realms, i.e. heaven, earth and the realms under the earth. We have seen that Jesus used His authority over the realms under the earth by releasing the Old Testament saints who were being held captive in death and taking them into heaven. We have also seen that until the end of the age that God has precluded Jesus from exercising His authority in two specific areas. Firstly, Jesus has been precluded from removing the devil and his angels from the earth. And secondly, Jesus has been precluded from enforcing His Lordship over mankind living on the earth.

Chapter 3
Our authority over the devil

Jesus delegated His authority

Ephesians 1:19-23 "and what is the exceeding greatness of His power toward us who believe, according to the working of His mighty power (20) which He worked in Christ when He raised Him from the dead and seated Him at His right hand in the heavenly places, (21) far above all principality and power and might and dominion, and every name that is named, not only in this age but also in that which is to come. (22) And He put all things under His feet and gave Him to be head over all things to the church, (23) which is His body, the fullness of Him who fills all in all."

In this section we want to discuss the fact that Jesus has delegated His authority in the earth today to His church, and what that authority encompasses. We have already seen that all authority has been given to the Lord Jesus. Nevertheless there is more to it than that, because in the above quoted passage of scripture the apostle Paul teaches us that God has placed all things under the feet of Jesus and given Him to be head over all things to the church, which is His body. So what does that statement mean? It simply means that the authority which Jesus has been given also extends to the church, which is His body. In other words every member of the body of Christ has the

Our authority over the devil

same authority that Christ has, for Paul goes on to teach us that the church has been raised up together with Christ Jesus and been made to sit together in the heavenly places in Christ, far above all principalities, powers, might, dominion, and every name that is named (Ephesians 2:6). The clear implication of Paul's statement is that all saints, both the saints in heaven and the saints living on the earth, having been placed over all things in Christ, are therefore partakers of Christ's authority over all principalities, powers, might, dominion, and every name that is named.

> *Luke 10:18-20 "And He said to them, "I saw Satan fall like lightning from heaven. (19) Behold, I give you the authority to trample on serpents and scorpions, and over all the power of the enemy, and nothing shall by any means hurt you. (20) Nevertheless, do not rejoice in this, that the spirits are subject to you, but rather rejoice because your names are written in heaven."*

The context of the above quoted passage of scripture is that Jesus had sent the disciples out to preach the gospel; before sending them out however, the Lord gave them power to cast out demons and heal the sick. On their return the disciples excitedly informed the Lord that even the demons were subject to them in His name, and so our Lord's response to that statement is recorded in this passage. The point that I want to highlight from this passage however, is that the Lord Jesus confirms to us that He has given His church authority over serpents and scorpions and over all the power of the enemy. Jesus went on to explain who the serpents and scorpions i.e. our enemy are, for He told us that the spirits are subject to us.

Our authority over the devil

In other words because of the authority which the Lord Jesus has given to His church, Satan and his entire realm of demons are now subject to the saints.

> *Matthew 28:18-20 "And Jesus came and spoke to them, saying, "All authority has been given to Me in heaven and on earth. (19) Go therefore and make disciples of all the nations, baptizing them in the name of the Father and of the Son and of the Holy Spirit, (20) teaching them to observe all things that I have commanded you; and lo, I am with you always, even to the end of the age." Amen."*

In the above quoted passage of scripture our Lord Jesus confirmed the truth to us that all authority in heaven and earth has been given to Him. When Jesus made that comment however, He then immediately told the church to "Go therefore". In other words because all authority has been given to Jesus; as the Head of the church He expects the church to go out and exercise His authority in the earth. And really if the truth be told, if the church chooses not to exercise the Lord's authority in the earth then no one else will. So why is that? The reason is because the Lord Jesus, the Head of the church, is currently seated at the right hand of God the Father in heaven. And so it is only through the church, which is His body in the earth, that the Lord Jesus can accomplish the work of God in the earth today. When our Lord Jesus came to the earth in the flesh, the mandate given to Him by the Father was to destroy the works of the devil, which is exactly what He did wherever He went (1 John 3:8). That mandate has not changed just because Jesus no longer walks the earth in the flesh, for Jesus still walks the earth today through His body, which is the church. And so

Our authority over the devil

it is through the church that Jesus continues to fulfil the mandate of the Father to destroy the works of the devil. And the reason the body of Christ can do that is because it has been endued with the same authority which the Head has i.e. the authority of the Lord Jesus Christ.

To summarize; from our examination of the scriptures quoted in this section we have seen that because we are the body of Christ, the authority given to the Lord Jesus extends to the church as well. We have seen that the authority given to the church by the Lord Jesus is over the devil and all of his demons. We have also seen that because Jesus has delegated His authority in the earth to the church; that just as Jesus did when He walked in the flesh, the church is also mandated to destroy the works of the devil.

The believer's weapons

Mark 16:17-18 "And these signs will follow those who believe: In My name they will cast out demons; they will speak with new tongues; (18) they will take up serpents; and if they drink anything deadly, it will by no means hurt them; they will lay hands on the sick, and they will recover."

We have seen in the previous section that the Lord has delegated His authority in the earth to His church; the main purpose being so that they can destroy the works of the devil. And so in this section we want to discuss the two main weapons available to the saints, which they can use to enforce their authority over Satan and his demons. A useful analogy to explain the believer's interaction with the devil and his cohorts is to look at the interaction which

Our authority over the devil

takes place between police officers and criminals. Obviously in this analogy the police officer represents the believer while the criminal represents the devil. When police officers confront criminals, very often it becomes necessary for them to use force in order to subdue said criminals. And so in order to assist the police officers in subduing said criminals, the police officers have various weapons available to them, such as tasers and firearms for example. In a similar manner when believers confront demons, they too have certain spiritual weapons available to them in order to deal with said demons. In the above quoted passage of scripture Jesus taught us that the very first sign which would follow those who believe, is that they would cast out demons in His name. And so we see that the first weapon available to the saints is the name of Jesus. Clearly Satan and his cohorts are unable to resist the name of Jesus, for God has decreed that every knee must bow to that name. And so we see that demons are forced to obey any instruction given to them using the name of Jesus. In illustration of this point it is interesting to note that by using the name of Jesus, even unbelievers can exercise authority over the devil and his demons. For our Lord taught us that it will be revealed on the day of judgement that even those whom He has never known and who practiced lawlessness, were nevertheless able to cast out demons through the use of His name (Matthew 7:22). There is also the account of the apostle John mentioning to Jesus that, because they weren't the Lord's disciples, he and the apostles had stopped certain men from using the name of Jesus to cast out demons. Our Lord's response to John was that, even if they were not His disciples, the apostles should not prevent people from using His name (Luke 9:49-50). And so clearly if even unbelievers can exercise authority over demons using the

Our authority over the devil

name of Jesus, then how much more should the church, which has every right to the use of His name, do the same.

> *Matthew 4:3-11 "Now when the tempter came to Him, he said, "If You are the Son of God, command that these stones become bread." (4) But He answered and said, "It is written, 'Man shall not live by bread alone, but by every word that proceeds from the mouth of God.' "(5) Then the devil took Him up into the holy city, set Him on the pinnacle of the temple, (6) and said to Him, "If You are the Son of God, throw Yourself down. For it is written: 'He shall give His angles charge over You,' and, in their hands they shall bear You up, lest You dash your foot against a stone.' "(7) Jesus said to him, "It is written again, 'You shall not tempt the Lord your God.' "(8) Again, the devil took Him up on an exceedingly high mountain and showed Him all the kingdoms of the world and their glory. (9) And he said to Him, "All these things I will give You if You will fall down and worship me." (10) Then Jesus said to him, "Away with you, Satan! For it is written, 'You shall worship the Lord your God, and Him only you shall serve.' "(11) Then the devil left Him, and behold, angels came and ministered to Him."*

Just as the saints have access to the name of Jesus; so it is that they also have access to the word of God. The bible refers to the word of God as being the sword of the Spirit (Ephesians 6:17). And so we see that the second spiritual weapon available to the saints is the word of God. This is another weapon which Satan and his demons have no ability to withstand. So how should the saints use this weapon? In the above quoted passage of scripture we see

Our authority over the devil

that every time Satan tried to tempt the Lord Jesus, He would counter the devil's temptation with the words "it is written". In other words Jesus countered every temptation by quoting God's word on the subject. And so we see that by quoting the word of God, that eventually the devil was forced to depart from Jesus. But I want you to notice that the devil also knows God's word, for in this passage we see the devil quoting the bible to Jesus. Nevertheless we can see from this passage that when the devil quotes God's word that he distorts it, for even though it was true that God had given His angels charge over Jesus, it would have been presumptuous of the Lord to cast Himself off the temple roof just to prove it. And so Jesus countered the devils' distortion by correctly quoting God's word on the subject. We see a principle here; which is that when Satan quotes God's word he distorts it in an attempt to persuade the believer to act presumptuously and thus commit sin. And so we see from this account how the saints should use the sword of the Spirit against the devil and his demons. Whenever saints encounter any form of demonic attack then they should quote to the devil what God's word says about the subject in question. And if the devil attempts to respond by distorting God's word, then the saints should counter that distortion with the correct rendering of God's word on the subject.

To summarize; from our examination of the scriptures quoted in this section we have seen that there are two main weapons made available to the saints which they can use to enforce their authority over the devil and his demons. The first weapon is the name of Jesus and the second is the word of God. We have also seen how the saints should use these weapons against the devil and his demons.

Our authority over the devil

We must exercise our authority

Ephesians 6:11-17 *"Put on the whole armour of God that you may be able to stand against the wiles of the devil. (12) For we do not wrestle against flesh and blood, but against principalities, against powers, against the rulers of the darkness of this age, against spiritual hosts of wickedness in the heavenly places. (13) Therefore, take up the whole armour of God that you may be able to withstand in the evil day, and having done all, to stand. (14) Stand therefore, having girded your waist with truth, having put on the breastplate of righteousness, (15) and having shod your feet with the preparation of the gospel of peace; (16) above all, taking the shield of faith with which, you will be able to quench all the fiery darts of the wicked one. (17) And take the helmet of salvation, and the sword of the Spirit, which is the word of God."*

We have seen in an earlier section that our Lord Jesus has delegated His authority in the earth to His church. And so in this section we want to discuss what the church is expected to do with that authority. In the natural when authority is delegated to an individual then that person is expected to exercise that authority. For example, a police officer is given authority to enforce the laws of the land. And so if a police officer is confronted with a member of society that is breaking the law, such as stealing a vehicle for example, it is expected of that police officer to arrest the individual and stop them from breaking the law. We would think it very strange if we saw a police officer in that situation telling the person stealing the vehicle that he was going to call the police. The reason

Our authority over the devil

we would think it strange is because he is the one who is meant to arrest the criminal, for he has that authority. In the spirit that principle remains the same, for the church has been given the authority of the Lord Jesus in the earth and it is expected of us to use that authority. What that means is that when we are confronted by the devil in any situation then we are to deal with him ourselves, because we have been given that authority. In the above quoted passage of scripture the apostle Paul admonishes the saints to stand against the wiles of the devil. In other words no one else is going to stand against the devil for us; because heaven has given us the authority and it is expected of us to exercise that authority and give no place to the devil in our lives.

1 Peter 5:8-9 "Be sober, be vigilant; because your adversary the devil walks about like a roaring lion, seeking whom he may devour. (9) Resist him, steadfast in the faith, knowing that the same sufferings are experienced by your brotherhood in the world."

In the above quoted passage of scripture the apostle Peter teaches us the same principle that Paul does i.e. the saints are expected to use their authority over the devil; for in this passage he tells the saints to resist the devil. The reason that Peter tells us to resist the devil is because we have been given authority over the devil, and it is therefore expected of us to use that authority. In other words no one else is going to resist the devil for us.

James 4:7 "Therefore submit to God. Resist the devil and he will flee from you."

Our authority over the devil

Scripture teaches us that out of the mouth of two or three witnesses we are to let every word be established (2 Corinthians 13:1). We have seen what Peter and Paul have said on the subject, and in the above quoted passage of scripture we see that the apostle James teaches the exact same thing; for in this passage James teaches us that it is up to the saint to resist the devil. The reason that James instructs us to resist the devil is because we have been given authority over the devil. And so we see that all three apostles teach the same truth i.e. the saints are expected to resist the devil. In other words God is not going to resist him for us, because we have been given all the authority we need to resist him ourselves. I want you to notice from this passage what happens when the saint does resist the devil, for the scripture says that he will flee from us. The reason that the devil flees from the saint who resists him is because the devil recognises the power of the one living on the inside of that saint and that power terrifies him, for he experienced that power when Jesus placed His foot on the back of the devil's neck.

To summarize; from our examination of the scriptures quoted in this section we have seen that it is expected of the saints to resist the devil for themselves. There is not one scripture in the New Testament that teaches the saints to get someone else to resist the devil for them, and the reason for that is because each saint has been given the authority they need to deal with the devil themselves.

Our sphere of authority

2 Corinthians 10:13-14 "We, however, will not boast beyond measure, but within the limits of the

Our authority over the devil

sphere which God appointed us--a sphere which especially includes you. (14) For we are not overextending ourselves (as though our authority did not extend to you), for it was to you that we came with the gospel of Christ."

In this section we want to discuss the limits of the authority given to each of the Lord's saints. Someone said, but I thought that we have been given authority over all the power of the enemy, so how can our authority have any limitations? While it is true to say that there is no limitation to our authority over the power of the enemy, nevertheless there is a limit as to where we can exercise that authority. In the above quoted passage of scripture the apostle Paul mentioned the sphere of authority that the Lord had given to him as an apostle. In other words Paul recognised that even though the Lord had given him authority as an apostle, that there was a limit to his sphere of influence where he could exercise that authority. This passage reveals a spiritual truth to us, which is that just like the apostle Paul, God has appointed to each believer their own sphere of influence in the earth and it is within that sphere that each believer is able to exercise their authority over the devil and his cohorts. The reason why, when dealing with the devil, is it important for saints to recognise their sphere of influence is because the devil ignores the saint who attempts to operate outside of their sphere of authority. In other words saints who attempt to operate outside of their sphere of influence will be unable to exercise authority over the devil and his demons.

Luke 10:19 "Behold, I give you the authority to trample on serpents and scorpions, and over all the power of the enemy, and nothing shall by any means

Our authority over the devil

hurt you."

The sphere of influence which God appoints to each believer begins with the individual believer themselves and extends outward from that point. In the above quoted passage of scripture the Lord Jesus taught us that He has given us authority over all the power of the enemy and that nothing shall by any means hurt us. In other words each believer has been given full authority to stand against any attempt made by the devil and his demons to harm the saint in any way.

1 Corinthians 11:10 "For this reason the woman ought to have a symbol of authority on her head, because of the angels."

The second sphere of influence over which saints are able to exercise their authority is in their home. In the above quoted passage of scripture the apostle Paul teaches us that the reason women wear a symbol of authority on their heads is because of the angles. The angels that Paul is referring to in this passage are Satan and his angels. The symbol of authority that Paul mentions in this passage refers to women covering their heads; which symbolises their submission to their husbands as their head and also as the head of the home. The point that I wanted to highlight from this passage is that Satan and his angels recognise the different levels of authority that God has decreed in the earth and will respond to that authority accordingly. The example given in this case is the authority that the man has as the head of his household, and also the authority that the woman has as his counterpart in that household. And so when it comes to the lives of their children, parents can and should exercise

Our authority over the devil

authority over Satan and his demons. Jesus also demonstrated a parents authority over their children when He instructed the ruler of the synagogue to stand in faith for his daughter so that she could be healed (Mark 5:35-36).

Matthew 8:5-13 "Now when Jesus had entered Capernaum, a centurion came to Him, pleading with Him, (6) saying, "Lord, my servant is lying at home paralyzed, dreadfully tormented." (7) And Jesus said to him, "I will come and heal him." (8) The centurion answered and said, "Lord, I am not worthy that You should come under my roof. But only speak a word, and my servant will be healed. (9) For I also am a man under authority, having soldiers under me. And I say to this one, 'Go,' and he goes; and to another, 'Come,' and he comes; and to my servant, 'Do this,' and he does it." (10) When Jesus heard it, He marvelled, and said to those who followed, "Assuredly, I say to you, I have not found such great faith, not even in Israel! (11) And I say to you that many will come from east and west, and sit down with Abraham, Isaac, and Jacob in the kingdom of heaven. (12) But the sons of the kingdom will be cast out into outer darkness. There will be weeping and gnashing of teeth." (13) Then Jesus said to the centurion, "Go your way; and as you have believed, so let it be done for you." And his servant was healed that same hour."

The next sphere of influence that believers have is over their employees. In the above quoted passage of scripture we have the account of the centurion who obtained healing from the Lord Jesus on behalf of his

Our authority over the devil

servant. And so we see that in this instance the servant wasn't healed through his own faith; it was through the faith of his employer. Jesus recognized the authority that the centurion had over his servant and therefore allowed his faith to be used for his servants healing. And so the tormenting spirit that was afflicting the centurion's servant had no choice in the matter, and had to obey the command of the Lord Jesus. That same principle applies today with believers who choose to exercise their authority in the lives of their staff. In other words when a believer exercises their authority in this area, Satan and his angels have no option except to obey.

Acts 5:16 "Also a multitude gathered from the surrounding cities to Jerusalem, bringing sick people and those who were tormented by unclean spirits, and they were all healed."

Believers also have full authority over demons that are affecting the lives of people who willingly come to the saints for deliverance. In the above quoted passage of scripture we see that everyone that came to the disciples to be delivered from the torment of unclean spirits were healed. The reason for that is because the individual that is tormented, in the act of coming to the believer for deliverance, is in that instance submitting themselves to the authority of the believer, thus allowing the believer to exercise their authority over the demon or demons that are afflicting them. And in that instance Satan and his demons also have no choice but to obey the disciple that exercises their authority in the name of Jesus.

Acts 16:16-18 "Now it happened, as we went to prayer, that a certain slave girl possessed with a

Our authority over the devil

spirit of divination met us, who brought her masters much profit by fortune-telling. (17) This girl followed Paul and us, and cried out, saying, "These men are the servants of the Most High God, who proclaim to us the way of salvation." (18) And this she did for many days. But Paul, greatly annoyed, turned and said to the spirit, "I command you in the name of Jesus Christ to come out of her." And he came out that very hour."

Another area where the believer has full authority over Satan and his angels is when they try to harass the believer. In the above quoted passage of scripture we have an account of a demon, which had possessed the slave girl, trying to publicly embarrass the Lord's apostles. In doing so, the demon opened the door for Paul to deal with him, and so Paul promptly obliged by using his authority to cast the demon out of her. Too late the demon found out that Paul was a believer that understood his authority in Jesus, and so the demon had to leave her. But I want you to notice that Paul didn't go looking for the demon to cast him out. So what do I mean by that statement? Everyone in town knew that this slave girl was a fortune-teller, including Paul. However, not everyone knew that the reason she practiced fortune-telling was because she was possessed by a spirit of divination. Although Paul knew that she was possessed, he nevertheless did not go to the place where she practiced fortune-telling to cast the demon out of her, because that would have been outside of Paul's realm of authority and he would have had no success and may have even landed up in some trouble. In other words Paul did not go looking to pick a fight with the devil in his own domain.

Our authority over the devil

Luke 10:18-20 "And He said to them, "I saw Satan fall like lightning from heaven. (19) Behold, I give you the authority to trample on serpents and scorpions, and over all the power of the enemy, and nothing shall by any means hurt you. (20) Nevertheless, do not rejoice in this, that the spirits are subject to you, but rather rejoice because your names are written in heaven."

There is one more area which falls outside the saints' sphere of influence and over which they cannot therefore exercise authority. In the above quoted passage of scripture our Lord clearly tells us that He has given us authority over all the power of the enemy. The church's enemy is Satan and all of his demons, for the scripture teaches us that we wrestle not against flesh and blood, but against principalities, against powers, against the rulers of the darkness of this age, against spiritual hosts of wickedness in the heavenly places. (Ephesians 6:12). In other words men are not the church's enemy and the church does not wrestle against them, but rather the church is called to walk in love toward men. Our Lord confirmed that truth in this passage by telling us that the spirits are subject to us. The spirits that our Lord is referring to in this passage are all of the unclean spirits that form part of Satan's kingdom. And so we see that although the church has authority over Satan and his entire kingdom, believers do not have authority over men in the earth. That agrees with the point that we mentioned earlier when we said that God will not override the free will of men in the earth. And so God does not give the church authority over men in the earth, for then the church would be able to exercise authority over their free wills, and God will not allow that.

Our authority over the devil

To summarize; from our examination of the scriptures quoted in this section we have seen that even though the saints have been given full authority over all of the power of the enemy, they are constrained to exercising that authority in their appointed spheres of influence. The first sphere is the individual themselves. The second sphere is their home. The third sphere is their place of work. The fourth sphere of authority would be over people seeking deliverance from demonic oppression. The fifth sphere of authority would be in response to direct demonic harassment. We have also seen that believers should not go uninvited into the devil's domain and attempt to exercise their authority. And then finally we have seen that the church has no authority over men in the earth.

Resisting the devil

Luke 22:31-32 "And the Lord said, "Simon, Simon! Indeed, Satan has asked for you, that he may sift you as wheat. (32) But I have prayed for you; that your faith should not fail; and when you have returned to Me, strengthen your brethren."

In this section we want to discuss what it means to resist the devil. We saw earlier, that the apostles Paul, Peter and James all said the same thing when it came to dealing with the devil; they all said that we were to resist him. So what does it mean to resist the devil? From time to time Satan will bring adversity into the lives of the saints in order to test their faith. The sole purpose of the adversity is to persuade the saint to draw back from appropriating the promises of God, and if possible to even

Our authority over the devil

persuade the saint to draw back completely from following Christ. In the above quoted passage of scripture our Lord Jesus revealed to us what transpires in the spirit realm when Satan brings adversity into the lives of the saints, for in this account our Lord revealed to Peter that Satan had asked for permission to sift him as wheat. And so in effect Satan had asked to test Peter's faith, for our Lord said that He had prayed that Peter's faith would not fail in his test. This account reveals to us that Satan cannot do as he pleases in the lives of believers, for he has to ask permission from God before he can test the saints. Nevertheless, even if God does allow the devil to test our faith we know that God is faithful, who will not allow us to be tested beyond that which we are able (1 Corinthians 10:13). We all know what transpired in the incident of Peter's test; he denied the Lord Jesus three times. And so on the surface it seems as if Peter failed his test; but that is not the case at all, for our Lord Jesus knew that Peter would deny Him and told him ahead of time that he would. What our Lord was more interested in was what Peter would do after he had denied the Lord, for that would be his real test of faith. We know that Peter wept bitterly when he realised what he had done; and so it would have been at that time that Satan would have done his utmost to persuade Peter to walk away from following Christ, by condemning him and accusing him of not being worthy to call himself a disciple of Christ. Nevertheless our Lord's prayer was heard and Peter's faith did not fail him, for he repented and returned to follow the Lord Jesus with an even greater zeal than he had before. In other words Peter resisted the devil and the devil was forced to depart from him. Our Lord Jesus has no favourites. And so when Satan asks the Father for permission to test our faith, our Lord Jesus still prays for

Our authority over the devil

each one of us that our faith will not fail, for He always lives to make intercession for each one of His saints (Hebrews 7:25). And so we can see from this account that resisting the devil means standing in faith in the midst of adversity.

1 Peter 1:6-7 "In this you greatly rejoice, though now for a little while, if need be, you have been grieved by various trials, (7) that the genuineness of your faith, being much more precious than gold that perishes, though it is tested by fire, may be found to praise, honour, and glory at the revelation of Jesus Christ."

In the above quoted passage of scripture the apostle Peter teaches us a number of truths about trials that saints incur in this life. Firstly, He teaches us that trials last for a period of time. In other words some trials can be of short duration while others can be of longer duration. Nevertheless in all instances heaven refers to the period of a trial as a 'little while'. And so even when trials last for a number of years, such as Paul's four years of imprisonment for example, in comparison to eternity they are still for a little while. The second thing that Peter teaches us about trials is that, in the natural, we will be grieved by our trials. In other words going through trials is not a pleasant experience. Nevertheless the saint that focuses on the end result of their trial can rejoice through it all, knowing that the outcome will ultimately glorify the Lord Jesus. And then finally Peter teaches us that in all instances the trial we are going through has come about with the sole purpose of testing our faith. And so we see that the saint that resists the devil by enduring their trial

Our authority over the devil

steadfast in their faith will eventually see the devil depart from them and the trial will come to an end.

James 1:2-4 "My brethren, count it all joy when you fall into various trials, (3) knowing that the testing of your faith produces patience. (4) But let patience have its perfect work, that you may be perfect and complete, lacking nothing."

In the above quoted passage of scripture the apostle James teaches us similar truths about the various trials that saints encounter in life. In this passage He tells us what attitude we should have when we encounter trials in life, for He tells us to be joyful in our trial. In the previous passage we saw that, in the natural, a trial is anything but a joyful experience. Nevertheless James teaches us that the reason believers are to consider their trial a joyful experience is because they know that the trial is working to their benefit, for it is only through trials that the fruit of patience can be developed. In other words the spirits of the saints become more fruitful through the trial, for one of the fruits of the spirit is patience (Galatians 5:22). Nevertheless James also teaches us in this passage that it is ultimately our faith that is being tested in the trial. And so we see that the saint that resists the devil by standing firm in their faith will eventually see the devil give up and depart from them.

To summarize; from our examination of the scriptures quoted in this section we have seen that the devil is the one who initiates adversity (trials) in the lives of believers with the express purpose of testing their faith. We have seen that believers who stand steadfast in their faith during their time of trial are in fact resisting the

Our authority over the devil

devil, and that eventually the devil is forced to depart from them thus bringing their trial to an end.

Using God's word

> *Luke 4:8 "And Jesus answered and said to him, "Get behind Me, Satan! For it is written, 'You shall worship the Lord your God, and Him only you shall serve.' "*

In a previous section we discussed the different spheres of influence over which saints could exercise their authority. We also discussed the two main weapons available to the saints in enforcing their authority over the devil, i.e. the name of Jesus and the word of God. And so in this section we want to discuss the different areas of life over which saints should exercise authority, and the importance of God's word in enforcing that authority. So why is it important for believers to know God's word in these areas? If the believer is ignorant of God's word in these areas then Satan will take advantage of the saint's ignorance and exploit them. As we discuss each area in turn I have quoted a passage of scripture that is pertinent for that area. Obviously there are many more scriptures in the bible that deal with these areas, but one scripture is sufficient to deal with our adversary. And so whenever believers are confronted by the devil in any of the following areas, they are follow the Lord's example in the above quoted passage of scripture, by commanding the devil to depart from them in the name of Jesus while quoting God's word on the subject. When believers do that in faith then Satan will depart from them every single time.

Our authority over the devil

Romans 6:14-18 "For sin shall not have dominion over you, for you are not under law but under grace. (15) What then? Shall we sin because we are not under law but under grace? Certainly not! ... (18) And having been set free from sin, you became slaves of righteousness."

The first area which we will discuss is the area of sin. Satan is called the tempter (Matthew 4:3). The reason Satan has that title is because he will always try to tempt believers to commit sin. Satan does that because he knows that if he is successful in tempting the saint then he gains a foothold in the life of that believer. Nevertheless because of the substitutionary sacrifice of our Lord Jesus in this area, believers are no longer subject to sin and can thus exercise their authority in resisting the devil's temptations. The above quoted passage of scripture teaches us that under the new covenant sin has no dominion over believers, and having been set free from sin they can now walk in righteousness. And so we see that whenever believers are tempted to commit sin then they should follow the Lord's example by quoting God's word on the subject i.e. "get behind Me, Satan! For it is written, 'sin shall not have dominion over you, for you are not under law but under grace."

Matthew 8:16-17 "When evening had come, they brought to Him many who were demon-possessed. And He cast out the spirits with a word, and healed all who were sick, (17) that it might be fulfilled which was spoken by Isaiah the prophet, saying: "He Himself took our infirmities and bore our sicknesses."

Our authority over the devil

The second area which we will discuss is the area of sickness and disease. One of the very many devices that Satan uses to test the faith of believers is through the use of sickness and disease. Nevertheless because of the substitutionary sacrifice of our Lord Jesus in this area as well, believers are no longer subject to sickness and disease, and can thus exercise their authority in resisting the devil's efforts to place sickness and disease on their bodies. The above quoted passage of scripture teaches us that Jesus has taken our infirmities and has born our sicknesses. Jesus did that for us when His body was scourged by the Romans before He went to the cross, for the scripture also tells us that by His stripes we were healed (1 Peter 2:24). And so we see that whenever believers are tested with symptoms of sickness and disease being placed upon their bodies, then they should follow the Lord's example by quoting God's word on the subject i.e. "get behind Me, Satan! For it is written, ' He Himself took our infirmities and bore our sicknesses."

Isaiah 53:5 "But He was wounded for our transgressions, He was bruised for our iniquities; the chastisement for our peace was upon Him, and by His stripes we are healed."

The third area which we will discuss is the area of worry and anxiety. Another favourite tool that Satan uses to test the faith of the believer is in the area of worry. For Satan knows that if he can get the believer to begin to worry about various issues in their lives that he can neutralize their faith from operating in those areas, for worrying is the complete opposite to faith. The above quoted passage of scripture teaches us that the

Our authority over the devil

chastisement for our peace was upon Jesus. In other words Jesus bore all of our anxieties when He went to the cross for us. In the garden of Gethsemane Jesus told His disciples that His soul was exceedingly sorrowful even to death (Mark 14:34). And so just as Jesus bore our sins and bore our sicknesses so He also bore our worries. The reason that Jesus did that was so that we can walk free from them. That is why the scripture teaches the believer to be anxious for nothing (Philippians 4:6). As believers we can walk free from all worry and we can walk in His peace, for again our Lord Jesus has taught us that He has given us His peace (John 14:27). And so we see that whenever believers are tested with thoughts of worry and anxiety then they should follow the Lord's example by quoting God's word on the subject i.e. "get behind Me, Satan! For it is written, ' the chastisement for our peace was upon Him."

Galatians 3:13 "Christ has redeemed us from the curse of the law, having become a curse for us (for it is written, "Cursed is everyone who hangs on a tree")."

The fourth area which we will discuss is the area of plundering and oppression. In describing our adversary, our Lord Jesus referred to him as the one who steals, kills, and destroys (John 10:10). God has stated that those who are under the curse of the law would be oppressed and plundered continually by their enemies (Deuteronomy 28:29). And so we see that as our enemy, Satan tries to oppress and steal from believers as much as he can. So how does he do that? One of the ways is that he influences people to act against the saints. For example, the saints may experience motor vehicle accidents or incidents of

Our authority over the devil

having things stolen from them, such as cell phones, etc. They may find themselves working for employers that begin to treat them harshly. Although in all of those instances it is people that are acting against the believer, nevertheless it is still the devil that influences those people to act in that manner. Another way that Satan attempts to bring destruction upon believers is through the use of the elements of nature, for you will recall that he used a tornado to kill Job's children (Job 1:18-19). Nevertheless as the scripture quoted above states, Christ has redeemed the believer from the curse of the law. Therefore believers are no longer subject to the oppression and plundering of our enemy. And so we see that whenever the devil attempts to plunder or oppress believers in any way, then they should follow the Lord's example by quoting God's word on the subject i.e. "get behind Me, Satan! For it is written, 'Christ has redeemed us from the curse of the law."

Matthew 18:18 "Assuredly, I say to you, whatever you bind on earth will be bound in heaven, and whatever you loose on earth will be loosed in heaven."

The fifth area which we will discuss is the area of opposition. Another way that Satan comes against believers is by placing stumbling blocks in their path. In other words believers may come across opposition when they attempt to do certain things, particularly things pertaining to the kingdom of God. Again, in all of these instances it is people that act against the believer, but nevertheless it is still the devil that influences those people to act in that manner. In the above quoted passage of scripture our Lord Jesus has given us the authority to

Our authority over the devil

bind the devil so that he cannot influence people to hinder us in our endeavours. You will recall that on another occasion our Lord taught us that in order for us to plunder the strong man's house (in context our Lord was referring to Satan), that we must first bind the strong man and then we can plunder his house (Mark 3:27). Also in this passage our Lord gave us the authority to loose whatever resources we may need, that the devil would try to withhold from us. And so we see that whenever the devil attempts to hinder the believer in their activities in any way, then they are to simply bind him in the name of Jesus, thus preventing him from influencing people from placing hindrances before the believer. In the same manner, whenever the devil attempts to withhold required resources from the believer in any way, then they are to simply loose those same resources in the name of Jesus, thus releasing those resources from Satan's control, to be made available to the believer. And so we see that in both binding and loosing the devil in the name of Jesus, Satan is rendered powerless to act against the believer in these areas.

Job 1:9-10 "So Satan answered the Lord and said, "Does Job fear God for nothing? (10) Have You not made a hedge around him, around his household, and around all that he has on every side? You have blessed the work of his hands, and his possessions have increased in the land."

There is one final aspect in this section that I want to discuss. There is a worldly saying "that prevention is better than cure". In the context of dealing with the devil that statement agrees with scripture, for the scripture teaches us that we are to give the devil no place

Our authority over the devil

(Ephesians 4:27). So what do I mean by that statement? Instead of reacting to the devil when he brings adversities into the life of the believer, believers should be vigilant in these areas by constantly confessing God's word over their lives and the lives of their households. In the above quoted passage of scripture Satan complained to God about the hedge of protection that God had placed around Job, which prevented Satan from gaining any access to Job, his household, or anything that he owned. Because of the authority given to the church under the new covenant, the saints are responsible for putting up their own hedges, thus preventing the devil from gaining any access to their lives, the lives of their households, and everything that they own. The saints put up hedges of protection in these areas by constantly confessing God's word over their lives, the lives of their households and everything that they own.

To summarize; from our examination of the scriptures quoted in this section we have discussed five main areas over which believers should exercise their authority i.e. sin, sickness, worry, plundering and oppression and then finally opposition. We also discussed the importance of using God's word effectively in dealing with the devil and his demons. And then finally we discussed the importance of the saints placing a hedge of protection around themselves, their households and all that they own.

Our authority over the devil

Chapter 4
Dealing with our adversary

Satan's devices

> 2 Corinthians 2:10-11 *"Now whom you forgive anything, I also forgive. For if indeed I have forgiven anything, I have forgiven that one for your sakes in the presence of Christ, (11) lest Satan should take advantage of us; for we are not ignorant of his devices."*

In order for the saints to deal effectively with the devil, it is important for them to understand the various strategies that Satan employs in his endeavour to overcome them. And so in this section we want to discuss the different devices that Satan uses in order to gain advantage over the saints. We have seen in this teaching thus far that all believers have full authority over the devil. Nevertheless we have also seen that Satan is the god of this world and that his aim is to exercise authority over all those who will let him. In an earlier passage of scripture which we quoted, the apostle Paul described our interaction with Satan and his realm as a wrestling match (Ephesians 6:12). If you have ever watched an Olympic wrestling match, you will understand the picture that the apostle Paul is trying to portray for us. In a wrestling contest the two opponents try to pin each other to the mat by gaining advantage over each other. And so that is exactly what our opponent tries to do to the saints, i.e. he

Dealing with to our adversary

tries to gain advantage over them. The way that Satan does that is by tempting the believer to commit sin, for he knows that if he is successful in that endeavour that he then is able to pin that saint to the mat, so to speak. In the above quoted passage of scripture the apostle Paul reveals one of the devices that Satan uses, which is to tempt the believer to walk in unforgiveness. Clearly from this passage we can see that if the believer were to fall into that trap, that their adversary would be able to gain advantage over them. In other words Satan would pin them to the mat and they would become ineffectual in being able to exercise their authority over him.

> Ephesians 4:26-27 "Be angry, and do not sin": do not let the sun go down on your wrath, (27) nor give place to the devil."

In the above quoted passage of scripture the Holy Spirit through the apostle Paul reveals to us just how we can give place to the devil in our lives. Clearly it is through the avenue of sin that Satan gains advantage over believers. And so it is our responsibility to ensure that we give no place to the devil by avoiding his temptation to commit sin. For it is when we choose to resist the devils temptation to sin that we are then able to exercise our full authority over him and his demons. In other words we are able to pin the devil to the mat.

> 2 Timothy 2:24-26 "And a servant of the Lord must not quarrel but be gentle to all, able to teach, patient, (25) in humility correcting those who are in opposition, if God perhaps will grant them repentance, so that they may know the truth, (26) and that they may come to their senses and escape

Dealing with to our adversary

the snare of the devil, having been taken captive by him to do his will."

In the above quoted passage of scripture the apostle Paul is not describing the status of unbelievers, but rather he is describing the condition of saints that had been taken captive by Satan to do his will. This passage declares that they had become ensnared by the devil and the reason that happened was because they submitted to the devil's temptation to walk in sin. In context, these particular disciples had begun to teach false doctrine in the church. And so it was because they were walking in sin that they needed the mercy to God to grant them repentance. Nevertheless until that happened, these disciples had been taken captive by their adversary. In other words Satan had them pinned to the mat and they had become completely ineffectual in being able to exercise their rightful authority over the devil.

1 John 5:18 "We know that whoever is born of God does not sin; but he who has been born of God keeps himself, and the wicked one does not touch him."

In the above quoted passage of scripture the Holy Spirit through the apostle John teaches us how to walk so that our adversary cannot gain advantage over us. He simply teaches us to stay away from sin, for He tells us that whoever is born of God does not sin. Satan knows that sin opens the door for him and so he will always try tempting the believer to commit sin. That's exactly what he did to Jesus and we are no different. But this same passage teaches us that he who is born of God keeps himself. The word translated "keep" can also be translated

Dealing with to our adversary

"to guard". In other words believers that guard themselves and stay away from temptation so that they do not walk in sin, keep the door closed on Satan. For the scripture says that the wicked one does not touch them. In other words Satan cannot put sickness on their bodies, he cannot steal from them and he cannot bring destruction into their lives.

To summarize; from our examination of the scriptures quoted in this section we have discussed how the devil tries to gain advantage over the saints by tempting them to commit sin. We have seen that if Satan is successful in tempting the saint to commit sin then he is able to nullify their ability to exercise their rightful authority over him. We have also seen that the devil is unable to touch the saint that resists his temptation to commit sin, because of which the saint is able exercise their rightful authority over him.

Satan is persistent

> Luke 4:13 "Now when the devil had ended every temptation, he departed from Him until an opportune time."

In this section we want to discuss the devil's persistence in his war against the saints. Until Jesus returns and Satan is bound by the angel for one thousand years, our adversary is not going to go away, for as we have already seen, he is the god of this world and as such he has every right to be here. The saints on the other hand are citizens of heaven, and so technically speaking we are on foreign soil while we live in this world. In other words just as our Lord Jesus is from above and not of this world,

Dealing with to our adversary

neither are we of this world (John 8:23). The point is; even though we exercise authority over the devil while we are on the earth, we do not have the authority to banish him from our lives altogether. And so what we will find is that when we do exercise our authority over the devil forcing him to depart from us, nevertheless after a period of time has elapsed he will return to test the believer once again. In the above quoted passage of scripture we see that the same thing happened to the Lord Jesus when He walked the earth, for the scripture says that the devil departed from Him until an opportune time. In other words when our Lord instructed Satan to depart from Him that is exactly what Satan did, but at a later time the devil came back and once again tried to tempt the Lord Jesus. And so if Satan returned to tempt the Lord Jesus, then we are no different and we can expect that the devil will return from time to time to tempt the believer once again. Nevertheless, each time that Satan returns we are to simply exercise our authority over him and he will once again depart from us.

To summarize; from our examination of the scripture quoted in this section we have discussed the fact that as the god of this world that the devil has every right to be here. We have seen that because we cannot banish the devil from our lives entirely that he will return from time to time to test the saints once again.

Satan is a dignitary

Jude 1:8-9 "Likewise also these dreamers defile the flesh, reject authority, and speak evil of dignitaries. (9) Yet Michael the archangel, in contending with the devil, when he disputed about

Dealing with to our adversary

the body of Moses, dared not bring against him a reviling accusation, but said, "The Lord rebuke you!"

In this section we want to discuss the fact that Satan is a dignitary, and how that impacts the saint's interaction with him. In the above quoted passage of scripture the apostle Jude refers to Satan and his angels as dignitaries. So what does that statement mean? It simply means that even though Satan is a fallen angel, he nevertheless still carries the authority that was originally given to him by God. In explaining the concept of dealing correctly with even fallen authorities, the apostle Jude teaches us how Michael the Archangel confronts the devil, by telling us that Michael dares not bring against the devil a reviling accusation, but rather says "The Lord rebuke you!". Because believers are in Christ they have a higher level of authority than angels. And so when believers address the devil they would not say "The Lord rebuke you", but rather they would say "I rebuke you in the name of Jesus". Nevertheless the main point that I wanted to address from this passage is that in context, Jude is speaking about foolish individuals speaking evil of and reviling Satan and his angels. The apostle Peter speaks in a similar manner when he says that these people despise authority, are presumptuous, self-willed, not afraid to speak evil of dignitaries; while angels, who are greater in power and might, do not bring a reviling accusation against them before the Lord (2 Peter 10-11). So what does it mean when the scripture says that these individuals bring a reviling accusation against the devil? For example, I have heard ministers of the gospel displaying their ignorance in this area by referring to Satan as a worm or as an idiot. Such statements would be classified as bringing a reviling accusation against him. Satan himself

Dealing with to our adversary

has no problem with foolish individuals who revile him, precisely because it plays into his hands. Because as the accuser of the brethren, Satan then has the legal right to ask for access to the lives of those believers, and that does not bode well for them.

> *Romans 13:1-2 "Let every soul be subject to the governing authorities. For there is no authority except from God, and the authorities that exist are appointed by God. (2) Therefore, whoever resists the authority resists the ordinance of God, and those who resist will bring judgment on themselves."*

The context of the above quoted passage of scripture is speaking about governments that exist in the natural. Nevertheless the same principle regarding authorities in the natural also applies to the spirit realm, for God has created all authorities, both in the natural and in the spiritual realm. We have already seen that believers are not subject to Satan's authority, but at the same time we do not revile his authority. And so in that light we can read this passage by replacing the word "resist" with the word "revile", i.e. "there is no authority except from God, and the authorities that exist are appointed by God. Therefore, whoever reviles the authority reviles the ordinance of God, and those who revile will bring judgment on themselves." And so we see that as believers, we can refer to Satan even as our Lord Jesus referred to him, i.e. a liar, a thief, a murderer, a deceiver and whatever other description is given to him in scripture. Nevertheless we do not refer to him as a worm or as an idiot, for that is one and the same as bringing a reviling accusation against him, thus opening the door for Satan to bring judgement into the life of that believer.

Dealing with to our adversary

To summarize; from our examination of the scriptures quoted in this section we have discussed the fact that Satan and his angels, though fallen, are nevertheless invested with the authority given to them by God. We have seen that because these angelic beings have authority given to them by God that it is unwise for the saints to revile them, for doing so opens the door for Satan and his angels to inflict judgement on them.

If you believe you can receive Jesus as your Lord and Saviour by praying this prayer

Dear Heavenly Father,

I come to You in the Name of Jesus.

Your Word says, "the one who comes to Me I will by no means cast out" (John 6:37), so I know You won't cast me out, but You take me in and I thank You for it. You said in Your Word, "Whoever calls on the name of the lord shall be saved." (Romans 10:13). I am calling on Your Name, so I know that You save me right now. You also said, "If you confess with your mouth the Lord Jesus and believe in your heart that God has raised Him from the dead, you will be saved. (10) For with the heart one believes unto righteousness, and with the mouth confession is made unto salvation" (Romans 10:9-10). I believe in my heart Jesus Christ is the Son of God. I believe that He was raised from the dead for my justification, and I confess Him now as my Lord. Because Your Word says, "with the heart one believes unto righteousness," and I do believe with my heart, I have now become the righteousness of God in Christ Jesus (2 Cor. 5:21) . . .

And I am now saved!

Thank You, Lord!

Welcome to the family of God. Now that you are His child you need to read your bible (especially the New

Testament) daily, spend time in prayer daily and join a local church that will teach you to be filled with the Holy Spirit with the evidence of speaking in other tongues, so that you can grow spiritually. You also need to tell others how Jesus has saved you so that they too can be saved.

About the Author

From childhood, Michael E.B. Maher has always known that the Lord's call was upon his life for the ministry. When he was saved at the age of twenty-two, almost immediately the Lord Jesus began to deal with him about entering the ministry. However, it was only many years later that he committed to the Lord to answer the Lord's call to the ministry. And so, in 2014 Michael Maher Ministries was begun. From the beginning, the mandate given to Michael from the Lord Jesus was to preach the word. And so, this ministry preaches the word of God on every available platform around the world.

Michael Maher Ministries

Free Subscription

Join hundreds of others from countries around the world and read our Daily Bible Teaching Email and more, that will help you to grow in your walk with the Lord Jesus.

Thank you, sir, for helping me to understand these teachings clearly! Amen

- *Tawanda Masvina*

Amen to keeping on keeping on. Thank you for today's lesson. We must never forget to pray regularly and immerse ourselves in the Word – "a page (or Chapter) a day helps keep Satan at bay".
Blessings,

- *John Lombard*

Thank you so much for today's inspiration. This made so much sense to me and helped me overcome a huge block in my understanding.
Blessings and love

- *Pam Laughton*

Log on to our website to subscribe.

www.mebmaher.wixsite.com/website

Michael Maher Ministries

Online Bible Courses

Our courses are designed to help believers grow in their faith and reach their full potential in Christ that God intended for their lives, through the study of His word.

Flexible

Enrol any time: choose your topic of study; study at your own pace.

Affordable

Pay as you go.

Log on to our website to register.

www.mebmaher.wixsite.com/website

Michael Maher Ministries

46 Penguin Road
Pringle Bay, 7196
South Africa
Phone: +27 082-974-3599

On the Web

www.mebmaher.wixsite.com/website

www.ingramcontent.com/pod-product-compliance
Lightning Source LLC
Chambersburg PA
CBHW071309040426
42444CB00009B/1939